# Understanding Your Child's Sensory Signals

Keep it Real.  Keep it Simple.  Keep it Sensory.

## **Plus** Sensory in a Nutshell!

Angie Voss, OTR

Copyright © 2011 Angie Voss, OTR

3r<sup>d</sup> Edition 2015

ASensoryLife.com

ISBN-13: 978-1466263536
ISBN-10: 1466263539

**Dear Reader:**

It is my hope that as you read this book you will feel as though you're sitting with me at my kitchen table sharing a cup of coffee and talking about your precious child. To get that casual conversational feeling, I have taken grammatical liberties that would make my high school English teachers (and my editors) get out the red pen. The thing is . . . I write the way I talk. . . . not in the informational textbook style. So if I don't have perfect subject/verb agreement or correct pronoun usage, please know that this is what works for me, and I hope it works for you, as well.

## How to Use This Handbook

**Table of Contents:** The table of contents provides a list of the sensory signals discussed in the book. There are two signals listed per page.

**Sensory Signal:** The title of each page describes the sensory difference ("signal") that a child may be displaying. This signal is your cue that an adaptation, modification, or increase/decrease in sensory input is likely being indicated.

**Ideas to Help:** This handbook is intended to be user-friendly, so try not to over think each item. If the sensory signal applies, dive right into the "Ideas to Help" section! The suggested ideas are beneficial to all children and cannot be harmful in any way.

This handbook was written and intended to work hand in hand with **ASensoryLife.com**. Almost every topic you read about will have further information provided on the website. Use the website to support your understanding and application of the techniques discussed in this handbook. On the website you will find pictures, how-to videos, definitions, printable handouts, and links and ideas for specific sensory tools and equipment. Once on the website, utilize the search bar on the home page and simply enter the word or words you would like to learn more about!

## <u>DISCLAIMER AND RELEASE OF LIABILITY</u>

The activities and suggestions in this book are not a replacement for direct therapy intervention. Please consult an occupational therapist as necessary. The activities in this book require adult supervision, and safety is the first priority. The suggestions offered in this handbook are beneficial for all children, although modifications may need to be made based on the child's abilities and limitations.

Contents

### Standing or Walking in Line with a Group Causes Fear, Aggression, or Agitation

**Sensory Explanation**: This can be due to sensory defensiveness and an over-responsive tactile system, which creates a fight or flight response. Standing or walking in line involves frequent bumps and unexpected light touch. The nervous system and brain perceive the tactile input as dangerous and noxious, thereby responding in a defensive fashion. Also, other sensory factors may come into play, such as auditory/visual input and difficulty with self-regulation.

**Ideas to Help!**

- Allow the child to be at the front or the rear of the line only. This will decrease the chance of bumps and unexpected touch by 50%.
- Have the child wear compression clothing.
- Provide an oral sensory tool or fidget toy while standing in line.
- Allow the child to designate a personal bubble and space while in line so others know it bothers him/her to be touched or bumped, bringing awareness to those around the child.
- Use earplugs or noise cancelling headphones to help, as the proximity of sound can be a factor.
- Use a floppy hat or fisherman's hat to help decrease the visual input in this situation.
- If possible, provide deep pressure touch prior to the child's standing in line.
- Provide a good match as a stand in line buddy for the child - one who is not going to create further sensory distress.
- Access the printable handout on ASensoryLife.com to educate others on this topic. http://asensorylife.com/standing-and-walking-in-line.html

### Loves Rain Boots or Cowboy Boots

**Sensory Explanation:** Boots provide additional proprioceptive feedback to the feet and ankles. Not only is this feeling regulating, calming, and organizing, it also provides additional body awareness and can help with balance and walking. Wearing the boots can also help with self-regulation due to the additional proprioception.

**Ideas to Help!**

- Let 'em wear the boots!
- It's okay if the boots do not go with the daily attire or if it is not raining out. Try to let this battle go, and if they want to wear the boots, there's no harm done.
- Tight, long socks and/or hiking boots could be a good alternative if the rain boots or cowboy boots are not feasible.
- Provide frequent doses of deep pressure touch to the lower body.
- Encourage jumping, stomping, marching, etc.
- Encourage other joint compression and joint traction activities.

### Loves to Always Wear a Hat

**Sensory Explanation:** Wearing a hat decreases visual and auditory input; this is often very comforting to a child. It decreases social expectations for eye contact and social interaction since the child can hide under the hat somewhat. The hat also provides deep pressure touch and proprioception to the head which can be calming and regulating. It also provides a uniform and stable type of tactile input since the wind is not blowing the child's hair and causing the hair to touch the face, which can be bothersome.

### Ideas to Help!

- Let 'em wear the hat! If at all possible, let the child wear a hat anytime they wish.
- Having a few hats to choose from is a good idea, as the child may want the hat but only accept a certain hat on any specific day vs. other days.
- Provide frequent doses of deep pressure touch to the head and face.
- Earplugs, noise cancelling headphones, or sunglasses may help.
- Encourage head stands and joint compression to the head/neck.
- Encourage activities to invert the head.
- Have the child wear a hooded sweatshirt.

### Dislikes the Feel of Metal

**Sensory Explanation:** This is likely due to tactile defensiveness/over-registration and possibly auditory defensiveness. The feel of metal may be noxious and painful to the child's nervous system. The high pitched sound that often goes along with touching metal surfaces can also be a factor.

### Ideas to Help!

- Respect this feeling and honor it as real, i.e., truly uncomfortable and painful for the child.
- Limit the wearing of rings and jewelry as you do not want the metal you are wearing to be the reason your child does not want to hold your hand, hug you, or accept other affectionate touch.
- Discuss this with the child if possible and see if they can verbalize whether the reason is the feeling or the sound.
- If it is the sound factor, try noise cancelling headphones or earplugs.
- If it is the feel factor, offer frequent and regular opportunities with tactile play to help with tactile system processing.
- Use tight fitting compression gloves during times when metal exposure is increased (such as at the park).

## Does Not Like Having a Picture Taken

**Sensory Explanation:** There are quite a few sensory factors involved with having a picture taken. These include the multi-sensory experience of bright, flashing lights, increased auditory input of those trying to give verbal commands or being silly to make the child smile, as well as the increased tactile input of positioning/ posture and the use of props. Other reasons are more complex, involving the "all eyes on them" concept and the very uncomfortable eye contact that is demanded by the camera.

### Ideas to Help!

- Limit formal picture taking and realize that the expectations may simply be too much.
- Try action shots and natural shots instead, preferably during a favorite sensory activity, such as climbing a tree or visiting the park.
- If you must have a formal picture taken, make sure that the photographer has been briefed and educated about the sensory differences prior to the appointment.
- Prior to the picture taking, prep the nervous system with a good 15 minute dose of proprioception and vestibular input to help the child cope with the sensory demands.
- Bring along tools for sensory defensiveness to use before and after the picture taking, such as headphones, a hat, sunglasses, etc.
- Have the child wear compression clothing under the dress-up outfit, since it will likely be difficult for the tactile system with the new and uncommon input from a dress shirt, tie, etc.
- Have the photographer limit the direct interaction with the child and limit the verbal cues. Definitely do not let the photographer physically cue the child for posture and positioning.

## Avoids Certain Textures Such as Blankets, Rugs, Sheets, Stuffed Animals

**Sensory Explanation:** This can be explained by sensory defensiveness and an over-responsive tactile system. All of the above mentioned items involve various textures, and a child with tactile defensiveness has tactile receptors in overdrive. They detect the slightest change in texture; some may be pleasant, some painful and noxious.

### Ideas to Help!

- Respect the fact that the child does not like certain textures, including certain sheets and blankets. Let the child choose what feels best for his/her tactile system.
- Provide full body deep pressure touch in frequent doses.
- Encourage tactile play with various textures, using wet and dry mediums for hands, feet, and full body.
- Try a Lycra™ compression sheet as an alternative to regular sheets.

### Avoids Group Settings such as Parties or Play Dates

**Sensory Explanation:** Group situations are multi-sensory and more difficult to handle than one might expect. There are auditory, visual, and tactile components. Additionally, social interaction and communication skills are required. The combination of these challenges can be overwhelming. The child may be completely content to observe from a distance, and this is totally fine.

**Ideas to Help!**

- Prior to a group activity, prepare the child's nervous system with a 15 minute movement and heavy/hard work activity.
- Provide sensory tools such as earplugs, headphones, a hat, sunglasses, fidget toy, or oral sensory tool.
- Do not push the child to the limit. If he/she is showing signs of overstimulation, it is time to leave or take a break.
- Do not insist on eye contact or verbal communication. Let it happen naturally.
- If the child is happy just standing back and observing the group, allow it to be okay; it is a much better option than trying to talk the child into it.
- Compression clothing or a Bear Hug™ vest can be helpful for calming and regulating input and allow the nervous system to be more accepting of the multi-sensory experience.
- Start with very small groups such as one other child and parent, wisely choosing the parent and child who will be the best sensory match for your child.
- Make the group situation fun and sensory based, such as a trip to the park or a play date in the backyard.
- Start with group situations at home in a comfortable and familiar setting; the additional people provide plenty of new input for the child.

### Craves Spicy, Salty or Sour Foods and Flavors

**Sensory Explanation:** Spicy, salty, and sour foods can assist with self-regulation and levels of alertness for all brains. They can be calming or alerting, depending on the brain and the moment. Children with sensory differences tend to crave these foods and flavors even more. Another reason may be due to under-registration of taste and smell, creating needs and cravings for stronger flavors that the child can actually taste.

**Ideas to Help!**

- Let 'em eat spicy, salty, and sour foods, realizing that it might be very important for self-regulation and maintaining a ready state.
- Offer and provide these taste preferences during snacks and challenging times, e.g., studying for a test, doing homework, or having to sit through a church service.
- Try to incorporate and honor these preferences as often as you can with meals. It can be of great benefit for your child's ability to self-regulate.

## Always Wants to be Carried or Held

**Sensory Explanation:** A child who struggles with sensory defensiveness and an over-responsive nervous system may request to be carried in order to feel safe and secure. The deep pressure touch provided while being held is likely calming, regulating and helping the child to avoid fight or flight or sensory overload. Being held greatly decreases the likelihood of unexpected touch and interaction with others. Being carried also decreases the motor demands. If the child struggles with coordination and/or endurance, balance, overall muscle tone and strength, this decreases the challenge for the child.

### Ideas to Help!

- Since there may be various reasons and factors as to why the child wants to be held, it is important to assess this first.
- If the reason is a motor or balance challenge, then encourage the child to walk in situations involving a "just right" challenge. (A "just right" challenge is encouraging practice to help with developing the skill, yet not too overwhelming and frustrating for the child). If it is endurance related, offering this type of challenge is also a good idea.
- If the reason is due to avoidance of sensory input, use the sensory tools appropriate for your child such as headphones or compression clothing to help.
- Respect the need to be carried in challenging and overwhelming situations and hold the child if necessary, giving a nice, and firm, deep pressure hug without using words to try to calm. When they feel safe, secure, and ready to get down and explore again, they will.

## Affectionate Touch Is Resisted or Avoided

**Sensory Explanation:** This can be explained by sensory defensiveness and an over-responsive tactile system. Kisses and light touch are often unpleasant and possibly even painful due to the overactive tactile receptors. Affectionate touch might also be avoided due to olfactory input from the other person, such as too much perfume or a strong hairspray. It could also be the unexpected brushing of the other person's hair or the uncomfortable texture of the hugger's clothing that is painful to the child's tactile system.

### Ideas to Help!

- Respect this challenge and offer firm hugs and a tight squeeze instead of kisses and light touch.
- Have the child wear compression clothing, possibly a Bear Hug™ compression vest.
- Provide frequent doses of full body deep pressure touch.
- Provide a squish box or pillow cave.
- Play the steam roller game as a form of affection.
- Encourage tactile play with various textures.
- Avoid wearing perfumes and other strong-smelling products such as lotion or hairspray.
- If your child is able to verbalize what bothers him/her about affection, talk about it together in an accepting and understanding way so that you can determine the sensory triggers.

### Prefers Big Squeeze/Bear Hugs

**Sensory Explanation:** Big squeeze/bear hugs provide a great amount of full body deep pressure touch and proprioception. This is very soothing, calming and organizing for the nervous system, and it feels especially satisfying if there is difficulty with sensory processing and self-regulation.

**Ideas to Help!**

- Provide big bear hugs throughout the day. Hug, hug, hug, then hug some more!
- Have the child wear compression clothing.
- Provide frequent doses of full body deep pressure touch.
- Provide a pillow cave.
- Provide a squish box.
- Provide a weighted blanket or lap pad.
- Incorporate proprioception throughout the day as often as possible.
- Try a body sock or resistance tunnel.

### Wind Causes Fear

**Sensory Explanation:** Although perhaps taken for granted, wind can be quite the sensory experience, involving unexpected tactile input and various frequencies of auditory input. Perhaps the most difficult part is the fact that wind is unpredictable.

**Ideas to Help!**

- Respect the fact that there may be a true fear of the wind and painful stimuli is involving the tactile system and auditory system.
- Provide earplugs, noise cancelling headphones, sunglasses and long-sleeved clothing. This may help if the child must be outside when it's windy.
- If outdoors for a sporting event and the child is a spectator, allow him/her to wrap in a blanket.
- Have the child wear a hooded sweatshirt.
- Trying to talk the child through it is not going to be effective, so choose an alternative.
- A fight or flight response is very possible; act accordingly.

### Dislikes the Feeling of Paper Towels or Paper

**Sensory Explanation:** This is likely related to an over-responsive tactile system and/or an over-responsive auditory system. The texture of the paper towels or the paper may be very uncomfortable and even painful, including discomfort with the sound of the paper towel being crumpled or paper being moved around.

### Ideas to Help!

- Use noise cancelling headphones or earplugs as needed.
- Try to let the child wear tight compression gloves for schoolwork and when turning pages in a book.
- Use cloth towels instead of paper towels for drying hands.
- Bring along a hand towel when out in the community and using bathrooms.
- Try wet hand wipes as an alternative to the super-rough towels in public bathrooms and schools.

### Does Not Like Water in the Ears

**Sensory Explanation:** The inside of the ear is part of the tactile system, and the tactile receptors may be very sensitive to the light touch and unpredictable, moving sensory input from the water in the ears. Water in the ears also creates a unique auditory sensation which can be uncomfortable and often painful to a sensitive auditory system.

### Ideas to Help!

- Use swimmer's earplugs in the bath, shower or swimming pool.
- If your child does not tolerate earplugs, teach him/her how to cover and protect the ears tightly when water is poured over the head. Always give plenty of warning.
- Try baths instead of showers, as baths are often better tolerated.
- Use a swimming cap to cover the ears.

## Rubs Hands Together Quickly and Intensely

**Sensory Explanation:** Rubbing hands together in this way provides deep pressure touch and proprioceptive input to the hands and arms. It also gives a dose of vestibular input if it creates movement with the body. This technique can be very calming and regulating for a child. It can also prevent times of sensory overload.

**Ideas to Help!**

- It's okay to let 'em do this. Respect it as a sensory need.
- Encourage other proprioceptive activities throughout the day, such as those listed below:
  - Deep pressure touch to the hands and arms
  - Joint traction via hanging from a bar
  - Wheelbarrow walking
  - Theraband® activities including wrapping the Theraband® around the hands for pressure
  - Compression gloves
- Assess the situations when the child does this hand-rubbing most and respond accordingly, minimizing sensory stimuli as needed.
- Try vibrating toys or a vibrating pillow to increase the amount of tactile and proprioceptive input.

## Afraid of Raindrops

**Sensory Explanation:** If sensory defensiveness involving the tactile system is present, raindrops can be a threat to the nervous system. The feeling of the raindrops can be uncomfortable and even painful when they hit the skin, especially the face. Raindrops are unpredictable and move once they hit the skin, which is even more of a threat to the tactile system.

**Ideas to Help!**

- Respect the fact that there might indeed be a sensory component involved. Being aware and identifying this can be very helpful.
- Be sure to keep an umbrella in the car or in a backpack as a necessary sensory tool, even when it is sprinkling.
- If an umbrella is not available, be sure to allow for use of a coat or blanket to protect the child's body in the rain.
- Have your child wear long sleeve compression clothing on rainy days to help minimize the chances of raindrops hitting the skin.
- Try a floppy hat, fisherman's hat, or a hood as protection on rainy days.
- Encourage deep breathing prior to going out in the rain.

### Showers Are Avoided or Cause Fear

**Sensory Explanation:** If sensory defensiveness involving the tactile system is present, the feeling of the water coming from the shower can be a threat to the nervous system (somewhat like raindrops). The feeling of the water can be uncomfortable and even painful when it hits the skin, especially the face. The water from the shower hits the body in an unpredictable and random fashion and the drops of water move once on the skin, which can be a threat to the tactile system.

### Ideas to Help!

- If the fear comes from a concern of water in the eyes, let the child wear goggles in the shower!
- Change the flow of the water or replace the shower head for a softer flow. This can make all of the difference in the world.
- Do not insist on a shower if a bath is available. This forced experience in the shower can be deregulating to the nervous system overall and can create a fight or flight response, one that the brain will not forget.
- Use swimmer's earplugs to help if water in the ears is a trigger of discomfort.
- Encourage singing in the shower and even dancing a little...this can help the child self-regulate and tolerate the sensory input a little better.
- Have the child shower when the nervous system is at its best. Refrain from having a child shower when already having a tough sensory day.

### Rubs Zippers on Pillows

**Sensory Explanation:** Rubbing a zipper provides tactile feedback to the fingers. It also provides proprioception to the hand. It can be a type of fidget toy for some as a way to self-regulate. It can be used as a way to calm the child, most frequently when the child is sitting still or trying to fall asleep.

### Ideas to Help!

- Let 'em do it and respect the fact that it is likely to assist with self-regulation.
- Some children may do this so often that the zipper breaks. Please replace the pillow for them.
- Not all zippers are created equal. ☺ One zipper may not have the same sensory effect for the child. Let the child choose the pillow if it needs to be replaced.
- Use this sensory signal to guide you in choosing the right fidget toy at school. A little zippered-pocket book or coin purse will probably be the best.

### Over-reacts to Minor Cuts/Scrapes

**Sensory Explanation:** If the tactile system is defensive and over-responsive, a minor cut or scrape may feel very different for the child. The tactile and pain receptors are in overdrive, and therefore may create a different response and perception. An over-reaction may also occur if the child has difficulty with self-regulation and struggles with sensory modulation. Unexpected painful stimuli may cause a fight or flight response as well (this is out of conscious control).

**Ideas to Help!**

- Deep pressure touch to the wound will likely help dampen the sensory response.
- Provide full body deep pressure touch or a bear hug to assist in self-regulation.
- Respect the fact that the reaction to the injury is real and try not to minimize it.
- Encourage deep breathing and/or offer an oral sensory tool or gum to help the child re-group.
- Choose your sensory battles wisely. If the child wants a bandage on, so be it. The bandage will indeed dampen and decrease the amount of sensory input to the cut or scrape, no matter how tiny it is.

### Messy Hands Must Be Wiped Off Frequently During Meals

**Sensory Explanation:** This is likely due to tactile defensiveness and over-responsiveness of the tactile receptors of the hands. The hands have a very large number of sensory receptors, and when they are over-responsive and over-register, messy textures can be very uncomfortable, even painful. Sometimes the need to wipe off the hands during a meal is due to the multi-sensory experience. The child's nervous system simply cannot handle so many types of input at once (taste, smell, the feeling of food in the mouth, and the tactile input to the hands).

**Ideas to Help!**

- Provide a wet rescue towel at all meals, such as a wet wash cloth that is right next to the child, to be used whenever it is wanted or needed to wipe something off.
- Allow the use of utensils, even when they might not be necessary. Cut up a sandwich in to bite-sized pieces if needed, so that the child can use a fork to poke instead.
- Encourage texture based play activities for hands and feet. Start with dry textures, such as dry rice, lentils, beans, or sand. Work up to messy play textures.
- Use therapy putty, Play-doh® or Moon Sand™ prior to a meal to help dampen the nerve endings in the hand so that it tolerates the messy textures of the meal.
- Provide regular and frequent doses of deep pressure touch to the hands, especially prior to a meal.

### Holds It Together at School, Then Melts Down at Home

**Sensory Explanation:** The school day is full of multi-sensory input, placing great demand and stress on the nervous system. This is especially difficult for those who struggle with sensory modulation and self-regulation. The child tries so hard to follow the rules of the classroom and to please the teacher and staff, as well as meet the social expectations of peers. When the child returns home from a long day of stress on the nervous system, a child may simply need to melt down to let it all out in an environment where the child feels safe, is not judged by others and can be with those who love and respect the sensory differences.

### Ideas to Help!

- Respect this as a true sensory signal that the school day was overwhelming and incredibly challenging.
- Try not to lean towards the theory of "Why do they do this at home and not at school? Doesn't that mean they can control it?"
- Offer a sensory retreat to help unwind and unload the sensory input from the day.
- Provide an indoor swing such as a hammock or cuddle swing, as swinging in slow, rhythmical planes of movement can be very calming and regulating.
- Invert the head.
- Provide full body deep pressure touch.
- Provide opportunities for proprioception.
- Decrease the amount of stimuli for at least an hour when the child gets home from school.
- Refrain from chores, homework, and other demands during the after-school hour.

### Reacts to the Smell of Air Fresheners

**Sensory Explanation:** The olfactory sense is very powerful and can cause sensory overload and dysregulation in and of itself, especially for those with sensory defensiveness and over-register sensory input. Not only is the olfactory sense a possible trigger, but almost all commercial air fresheners are made of toxins and chemicals which can wreak havoc on the nervous system. These can trigger migraines and asthma attacks, among other problems.

### Ideas to Help!

- Use only essential oils and natural air fresheners in the home.
- Be acutely aware of air fresheners when out in the community, including those at school, daycare, and public bathrooms.
- Take nose plugs or a mask/filter for places where fragrance is out of your control.
- If possible, in settings where you can have some control (such as your child's classroom) suggest that the teacher remove the toxic air freshener and offer to replace it with something natural.
- When at a store, ask your child if there are bothersome smells. This helps to determine if smell is a trigger.

### Does Not Like the Sound of a Turn Signal in the Car

**Sensory Explanation:** If a child has auditory defensiveness or even vestibular defensiveness, the sound of the turn signal simply can be too much sensory input while riding in the car. Riding in a vehicle already presents multi-sensory input challenges, and at the same time it limits a child's ability to get the necessary types of input to help self-regulate. This can especially hold true for a child who struggles with sensory modulation.

### Ideas to Help!

- Offer earplugs or noise cancelling headphones in the car, making sure they are always available in the car. It may be a good idea to have two sets, leaving one set in the car at all times.
- Suggest the use of an MP3 player so the child can tune out the extra auditory input and instead help to regulate via calming, enjoyable music.
- Offer an oral sensory tool in the car.
- Remember that fidget toys can be helpful while in the car.
- Provide a weighted lap pad or vibrating pillow.

### Prefers to be with Animals Rather than People

**Sensory Explanation:** Animals in general have a calming and therapeutic benefit for us humans. Animals also do not place social demands and expectations upon people like other humans tend to do, such as making eye contact or certain verbal communication expectations. Animals operate on a sensory level, which (of course) creates a perfect match. Animals love unconditionally and are content simply being in your presence, without all sorts of human demands. Animals can provide very calming and regulating tactile input via petting, including proprioception if holding a pet in the lap or having a large dog lay over the legs.

### Ideas to Help!

- Respect this sensory signal and allow your child to spend as much time as desired with animals.
- When you interact with your child, try to mimic this type of interaction . . . just be with your child. Limit conversation, offer a hug, etc., interacting in a way that feels good to your child.
- If you notice that animals are very calming and soothing for your child, do your best to incorporate animals into the child's life as much as possible.
- Check into the options of getting a service animal.
- Offer a weighted blanket or Lycra™ compression sheet as a good alternative to pets.
- Utilize soft fabrics or stuffed animals that are soothing from a tactile standpoint.

## Socks and Seams Have to Be "Just Right"

**Sensory Explanation:** This is likely due to tactile defensiveness and over-registration of tactile input. The seam in the sock can feel as extreme as a razor blade to a dull nagging lump, yet either way the child is unable to tune out the irrelevant sensory input.

### Ideas to Help!

- Seamless socks are my first recommendation.
- Tight compression socks are my second choice since they are less likely to move.
- Respect this as a true sensory challenge and take the extra time to help get the socks just right to start the day.
- If your child does better without socks at all, go that route when possible.
- Apply deep pressure touch to the feet prior to putting socks on.
- Provide snug-fitting shoes.

## Face Washing Causes Distress

**Sensory Explanation:** The face is part of the tactile system and face washing can be uncomfortable or painful depending on the texture of the wash cloth and amount of pressure used for washing. This is likely due to tactile defensiveness and over-registration of the tactile receptors of the face.

### Ideas to Help!

- Let the child choose the wash cloth and also let him/her do the washing.
- Provide deep pressure touch to the face prior to face washing.
- Encourage tactile based play with various textures, both wet and dry.
- Wash with firm pressure, yet not too much pressure…let your child gauge this.
- Encourage singing songs, clapping hands or stomping to help give a regulating and distracting dose of sensory input.
- Make sure the mild soap you are using is a pleasing and acceptable scent for your child.
- Offer bubble mountain right before the face washing.

### Refuses to Walk Barefoot on Grass, Sand, or New Surface

**Sensory Explanation:** The feet have a large number of tactile receptors, especially the bottoms of the feet. New or different textures can be uncomfortable or painful to a child with tactile defensiveness or those who over-register tactile input. The changes of texture when walking through the grass or sand can also be a factor, as sometimes you step on a rock or something that pokes you while barefoot. This unpredictable input can cause a child to refuse to walk barefoot.

**Ideas to Help!**

- Respect this as something that is truly painful and uncomfortable. Let the child wear shoes or socks.
- Provide deep pressure touch to the feet on a regular basis.
- Encourage the child to work his/her way up to bare feet by wearing flip-flops or open-toed shoes.
- Encourage tactile play activities for the feet in small doses . . . dry textures first, working up to messy textures.
- Encourage very brief doses of barefoot walking, following right in your steps in a fun follow the leader fashion. This way you can discover possible changes in the terrain/texture and warn the child or avoid it.

### Too Much Force or Intensity Is Used When Handling Objects Such as Pencils or Handles

**Sensory Explanation:** This is likely due to under-registration of proprioceptive input and decreased proprioceptive feedback to the muscles and joints. If a child is unable to detect or sense the amount of pressure he/she is applying with the muscles and joints, then too much force or intensity may be used.

**Ideas to Help!**

- Encourage heavy/hard work activities for the arms and hands.
- Encourage wheelbarrow walking and hanging from a bar or jungle gym.
- Provide Play-doh®, Moon Sand™, or Thera-Putty™.
- Increase the grip diameter on the writing utensil.
- Encourage the use of a hippity hop ball.
- Increase overall full body proprioception and vestibular activities to help sensory registration.
- Provide regular doses of deep pressure touch to the arms and hands.
- Provide vibration to the hands and arms.
- Provide joint traction and joint compression to the arms.

## Constant Eye Movements Such as Rapid Blinking or Raising Eyebrows

**Sensory Explanation:** This signal can be explained in a few different ways. It is important to have the child's vision checked by a professional first, as well as possible neurological components which need to be ruled out. If all checks out okay, then this can be a way that the child is getting proprioceptive and visual input and feedback, and it feels good to them. It can be calming and regulating and possibly serve as a sensory anchor; the ever changing visual stimuli when doing this helps with self-regulation. This can also be done as a way to avoid eye contact or uncomfortable social interaction.

### Ideas to Help!

- Let the child do it...no harm done and it is not bothering anyone else. Just recognize it as a sensory signal or sensory anchor and that the child is likely trying to self-regulate.
- Encourage frequent doses of vestibular and proprioceptive input throughout the day.
- Limit screen time. Those who use visual input to self-regulate tend to gravitate towards screens, yet it is not beneficial to the brain.
- Play games making funny, very dramatic faces to help give more proprioceptive input to the facial and eye muscles.
- Encourage making funny faces in the mirror, e.g., dramatic and goofy.

## Always Keeps Hands in Pockets

**Sensory Explanation:** When your hands are in pockets you are getting proprioception and deep pressure touch to the hands and wrists; this is often very calming and regulating to the nervous system. A child may also do this to avoid interacting with the hands due to tactile defensiveness or sensory over-registration. If the hands are in the pockets, it decreases the possibility of touching something that may be uncomfortable or painful.

### Ideas to Help!

- Let 'em do it...it's not bothering anybody. ☺
- Try to refrain from telling the child to take his/her hands out of the pockets, and know that it is helpful for the nervous system.
- Encourage proprioceptive activities, especially joint traction and compression to the arms.
- Provide regular and frequent doses of deep pressure touch to the hands and arms.
- Provide a vibrating toy or pillow.
- Provide a weighted lap pad or weighted blanket.
- Try compression gloves.

### Hurts Others or Pets While Playing

**Sensory Explanation:** This may be due to under-registration of proprioceptive input and decreased proprioceptive feedback to the muscles and joints. If a child is unable to detect or sense the amount of pressure he/she is applying with the muscles and joints, then too much force or intensity may be used. And in turn, doing things with force helps the child feel the sensory input involving proprioception, therefore assisting in self-regulation.

### Ideas to Help!

- Encourage heavy/hard work activities for the arms/hands.
- Encourage wheelbarrow walking and hanging from a bar.
- Provide a pillow cave, squish box or weighted blanket.
- Set up an obstacle course involving heavy/hard work.
- Provide a mini trampoline, BOSU® ball, or hippity hop ball.
- Encourage frequent doses of proprioceptive and vestibular input throughout the day.
- Encourage the use of Thera-Putty™, clay, or Play-doh®.
- Be sure to talk about this with the child, helping them to be aware that he/she may be hurting the person or animal. The child is most likely unaware of the pain or discomfort being caused.

### Loves to Walk in Circles

**Sensory Explanation:** Walking in circles stimulates the vestibular system, in a different way than when spinning in tight circles. It can be regulating and calming for the nervous system, especially for children who crave movement and/or under-register vestibular input. It may also be a sensory anchor and assisting in self-regulation.

### Ideas to Help!

- Walking in large circles in okay, but too much tight spinning needs to be supervised.
- Increase the amount of vestibular input overall. An indoor swing would be ideal.
- Encourage the use of a therapy ball or hippity hop ball.
- Provide a BOSU® ball.
- Encourage inverting the head.
- Provide a mini-trampoline or outdoor trampoline.

### Craves Vibration

**Sensory Explanation:** Vibration stimulates the tactile receptors and provides proprioceptive input to joints/muscles. This type of input can be very helpful in self-regulation. It is also helpful for those who under-register proprioception and tactile input, as it can facilitate body awareness and provides sensory feedback.

### Ideas to Help!

- Encourage use of a vibrating device on arms, legs, hands, feet, and back…it's good for them.
- Do NOT let the child place the vibrating toy or device on the ears (which they tend to want to do).
- Provide a vibrating pillow or other handheld massager that vibrates.
- For a very young child, vibrating crib mattresses are available.
- Offer the use of vibration with a pillow cave or squish box.
- Encourage other types of tactile play, especially messy play if they enjoy it.
- Encourage other types of proprioceptive input such as heavy/hard work.
- Provide regular doses of deep pressure touch.

### Touches Surfaces/Objects Repeatedly That are Soothing

**Sensory Explanation:** This sensory signal is likely due to under-registration of tactile input as well as difficulty with self-regulation. Touching a surface or object that is soothing facilitates nervous system organization and can be soothing and calming. It may also serve as a sensory anchor for the child.

### Ideas to Help!

- Encourage various texture based play with wet and dry textures. Full body play is encouraged, such as sandbox play.
- Encourage messy play in the bathtub with foam soaps or pudding.
- Provide a fidget toy/object that meets the soothing needs of the child.
- Provide vibrating toys.
- Encourage plenty of play involving the power sensations.
- Provide deep pressure touch.
- Provide joint traction and joint compression.

### Unable to Identify Objects by Touch Only

**Sensory Explanation:** This skill requires tactile discrimination and proprioceptive awareness of the hands, in addition to the ability for the brain to process and interpret the information. The technical term for this skill is stereognosis. Difficulty with this skill may be due to an injury to the brain or difficulty with sensory integration.

### Ideas to Help!

- Provide opportunities for vibration to the hands and fingers.
- Provide texture-based play for the hands, with wet and dry mediums.
- Encourage play with Play-doh®, Moon Sand™, and Theraputty™.
- Provide a dry texture bin with rice, beans, or lentils and hide small objects in the bin such as an eraser, paper clip, or small familiar toy. Have the child close his/her eyes and try to identify the object by moving it around in the hands.
- Provide frequent doses of deep pressure touch to the hands and arms.
- Provide joint traction and joint compression to the arms and hands.

### Enjoys Talking and Singing to Self

**Sensory Explanation:** Talking and singing can be a sensory anchor for a child. It's very calming and regulating for the brain, especially when it includes repetitive and familiar phrases or songs. It can also be a technique to tune out auditory input that is not being filtered well by the auditory system.

### Ideas to Help!

- It's okay to let 'em do it, respecting it as a sensory anchor.
- If in an environment or setting where this is disruptive, offer noise cancelling headphones or an MP3 player with their favorite music.
- Limit auditory distractions in the home (turn the T.V. off).
- Encourage movement activities involving listening games and other auditory input...this will work on auditory processing skills.
- If the child seems to do this in times of stress or sensory overload, be sure to encourage the use of a sensory retreat.

## Does Not Respond to Hand-Over-Hand Teaching

**Sensory Explanation:** The brain in general does NOT respond to hand-over-hand teaching, and for our children with sensory differences there are additional triggers and factors that come into play when using the hand over hand technique. The child may be tactile defensive, and it is truly painful or uncomfortable to have someone's hands over theirs. The close proximity of the teaching individual can also be very uncomfortable for the child for various reasons such as personal space, eye contact, auditory input, olfactory input, etc. Perhaps the teacher has perfume on that is noxious to the child, or the hair is brushing against the child and is uncomfortable to the tactile system.

**Ideas to Help!**

- Refrain from hand-over-hand teaching altogether.
- Try the techniques of forward or backward chaining instead.
- Tactile cues are okay for some children (this is different than hand-over-hand).
- Prior to any new task or challenging activity, be sure to prep the nervous system and brain via the power sensations to be sure it is warmed up and ready.
- Modeling the task or activity is a great alternative…side-by-side with the child.

## Holds Urine or Bowel Movements and Refuses to Use the Bathroom

**Sensory Explanation:** This is a very complex skill for the brain, much more than one may think. This is different than a child being unaware of needing to go to the bathroom. The children that hold it until they can't possibly hold it anymore may have sensory triggers that cause fight or flight in the bathroom, or even possibly just one BAD experience in a public bathroom with an extremely loud automated toilet or hand dryer. It may also involve a psychological component of "losing part of body", which is why the child may prefer to go in a diaper/pull up/underwear. One other possibility is that holding it gives a sense of control…which is pretty common for children with sensory differences.

**Ideas to Help!**

- Assess the bathroom environment very closely…are there sensory triggers which are keeping the child from feeling safe in the bathroom? Too loud? Strong smells? Toilet seat too cold?
- Limit the use of public restrooms to avoid the unpredictable sensory input. If you must use them, go in first to assess the situation, and bring along sticky notes to place over the sensors of the automatic toilets and dryers.
- Try the use of a portable toilet in a safe place for the child, even in his/her bedroom is great. This will help the nervous system let the guard down to relax enough to go to the bathroom.
- Self-regulation is the key to this overall…so a lot of calming and regulating proprioception on a daily basis is very important.

### Elevators and Escalators Are Avoided

**Sensory Explanation:** This can be due to vestibular defensiveness or possibly gravitational insecurity. It may also be due to a lack of body awareness and decreased proprioceptive feedback; therefore, the feeling of being on a moving object and not feeling secure with the body in space can be uncomfortable or frightening.

**Ideas to Help!**

- Encourage swinging in various planes of movement and with the body in different positions, such as reclined back or lying on the stomach . . . swinging side to side, back and forth, and diagonals. Never force this; only use it in doses that are well tolerated.
- Provide an indoor swing for year-round use.
- Provide a hippity hop ball or BOSU® ball.
- Encourage jumping on a trampoline.
- Plan heavy/hard work activities throughout the day.
- When on an escalator or elevator, hug the child or provide some type of deep pressure touch to his/her body.
- Provide regular daily doses of full body deep pressure touch.
- Encourage deep breathing on a regular basis.

### Feet Leaving the Ground Causes Fear

**Sensory Explanation:** This can be due to vestibular defensiveness or possibly gravitational insecurity. It may also be due to a lack of body awareness and decreased proprioceptive feedback….therefore, when the child jumps or hops or even runs, the body feels lost in space which is a very scary feeling. This could also be due to poor balance or decreased protective reflexes, and the brain/nervous system knows this and will protect itself by not engaging in such activities.

**Ideas to Help!**

- Encourage swinging in various planes of movement and with the body in different positions, such as reclined back or lying on the stomach . . . swinging side to side, back and forth, and diagonals.
- Encourage marching, stomping, and walking on uneven terrain.
- Encourage using a hippity hop ball or mini trampoline with a stability bar.
- Provide therapy ball activities.
- Plan heavy/hard work activities throughout the day.
- Provide regular daily doses of full body deep pressure touch.
- Compression clothing, a Bear Hug™ compression vest, or a weighted belt can help with body awareness and proprioceptive feedback.
- Provide joint compression and joint traction to the lower body.
- Have an OT or PT assess protective reflexes.

### Smells Own Hair and Others' Hair

**Sensory Explanation:** Olfactory input can be very soothing and calming for the nervous system. It is a very powerful form of sensory input. Hair often has either a pleasant smell from hair products or it may have a unique-to-that-person type of smell that is comforting for the child. It may also be a way to familiarize themselves with a new person. One other sensory explanation could be a sensory anchor, and this is assisting with self-regulation.

### Ideas to Help!

- Respect this as a sensory signal and that it may be necessary to feel comfortable and secure in their environment or surroundings.
- Offer other olfactory input such as via essential oils on a stuffed animal or something soothing.
- Use this as a sensory signal that the child may be struggling with self-regulation and provide doses of sensory input from the power sensations throughout the day.
- Inform and educate the teachers and caregivers in the child's life so that they understand the sensory reasoning behind this.

### Dumps Toys Constantly

**Sensory Explanation:** Some children like to dump toys well past the developmental stage of dumping. This can be explained in a few ways. The child may purely enjoy the visual input from watching the toys dump. This can be similar to the way a child likes to watch spinning objects; it is soothing and regulating for the brain. The child may also crave the sound associated with the dumping of the toys, therefore seeking out the auditory input. One other explanation can be a sensory signal indicating sensory dysregulation and that the child is overwhelmed and simply unable to organize and engage in play in any other fashion.

### Ideas to Help!

- Decrease visual clutter and keep the home environment organized.
- Assess the situation to determine the most likely sensory trigger…Is it auditory? Is it visual enjoyment?
- Create a sensory-rich experience involving dumping, such as scooping sand or dry rice/beans and pouring into a water wheel or different toy in which the child can enjoy the visual input.
- Encourage regular doses of input via the power sensations throughout the day to assist in self-regulation.
- If it seems to be meeting an auditory need, encourage other auditory input such as listening to music, singing songs, metronome games, or playing musical instruments.

### Gets Car Sick Easily

**Sensory Explanation:** This is most likely related to vestibular defensiveness and difficulty processing vestibular input, especially if this becomes a greater problem on curving and winding roads or with frequent stop-and-go. This can also be intermittent and based on the child's state of regulation. If the child is already having a tough sensory day and is on the brink of sensory overload, the vestibular input in the car may be simply too much for the nervous system and put them over the sensory edge.

**Ideas to Help!**

- Cover side windows to decrease the amount of visual input, which can directly impact the vestibular system.
- Encourage the child to just listen to music or sing instead of reading or watching a screen.
- Provide an oral sensory tool such as a Camelbak® water bottle or other resistive oral tool.
- Provide chewing gum or sour hard candy to suck on.
- Take frequent breaks for stretching or stopping at the park to hang on monkey bars.
- Encourage deep breathing.
- Provide a weighted lap pad.
- Provide noise cancelling headphones or earplugs to decrease sensory input overall at times of dysregulation or sensory overload.
- Provide sunglasses and/or a floppy hat to decrease visual input.
- Switch the vent to recirculating so the child does not have to deal with smells from the outside air.

### Head Being Tipped Backwards Is Avoided

**Sensory Explanation:** This can be related to vestibular defensiveness and a difficulty processing vestibular input. This may also be due to a decrease in body awareness which creates limited ability to determine body in space, and this is a very scary and unpredictable feeling.

**Ideas to Help!**

- Encourage swinging in various planes of movement and with the body in different positions, such as reclined back or lying on the stomach . . . swinging side to side, back and forth, and diagonals. Do this in very small doses, and doses tolerated by the child. Never force it.
- On a large therapy ball, have the child lie on the back, slowly working towards a greater inverted angle.
- With the child sitting on your lap facing you, hold the arms and have him/her slowly tip backwards. Let the child decide how far back to go.
- Provide full body deep pressure touch in regular doses.
- Provide regular doses of proprioception throughout the day.
- Try letting the child hang over the edge of the couch while giving very firm support to the body.
- Encourage deep breathing prior to all vestibular activities.
- Provide joint compression and joint traction.

## Loses Balance Easily/Appears Clumsy

**Sensory Explanation:** This can be due to decreased registration of proprioceptive and vestibular input and overall processing of the vestibular system. This in turn creates difficulty with body awareness and body in space. This can also be explained by poor motor planning, muscle tone abnormalities (high or low), postural and pelvic instability and weight shifting difficulties.

### Ideas to Help!

- Encourage heavy/hard work activities throughout the day.
- Provide obstacle courses.
- Provide a pillow cave or squish box.
- Have the child wear compression clothing.
- Provide deep pressure touch in regular doses.
- Encourage swinging in different planes of movement.
- Encourage the use of a hippity hop ball or BOSU® ball.
- Have the child wear a weighted belt or weighted shoe pockets.
- Encourage climbing up slides.
- Schedule a PT consult to rule out other neuromuscular issues.

## Smells New and Unfamiliar People

**Sensory Explanation:** Olfactory input can be very soothing and calming for the nervous system. It is a very powerful form of sensory input and can help the child have a sense of control and understanding of a new person or situation. New people have new smells, some may be pleasant and some not so pleasant. This may be a technique that is the most comforting to a child in familiarizing themselves with a new person. One other sensory explanation could be a sensory anchor, and this is assisting with self-regulation.

### Ideas to Help!

- Respect this as a sensory signal and be sure to educate those in the child's life as to why the child does this and let them know it is important for self-regulation to allow them to do so.
- Please do not treat it as silly or weird...and do not let others do so, either.
- Assist with self-regulation by regular daily doses of input from the power sensations.
- Offer olfactory input via essential oils and other natural scents that the child finds soothing and calming.
- In new, unfamiliar, and challenging environments be sure that your child is prepared with sensory tools and strategies to help, such as an oral sensory tool, fidget toy, or noise cancelling headphones.

### Riding a Bike Is Difficult or Causes Fear

**Sensory Explanation:** Likely decreased registration of proprioceptive and vestibular input is present. This in turn creates difficulty with body awareness and body in space. Vestibular defensiveness may also be present, which can cause an over-reaction/response to the movement and balance changes involved in riding a bike. Another explanation may be poor balance or motor planning skills, as well as difficulty with bilateral integration. Visual perceptual skills can also be a factor, such as depth perception and/or visual scanning and convergence.

### Ideas to Help!

- Be sure the child is proficient with riding a tricycle before attempting a two-wheeler, even with training wheels. It is important that the child be able to independently pedal and steer before working on the balance factor.
- Balance bikes are a great alternative and starting point.
- Once on a two-wheeler, allow use of the training wheels as long as needed. Do not force the issue of going without training wheels until the child is truly ready.
- Prior to practicing riding the bike, have the child engage in a movement and heavy/hard work activity for 10-15 minutes.
- Encourage deep breathing before, during, and after. Bubble mountain would be a great activity before practicing biking.
- Tandem bikes can be helpful in learning the weight shifting of the pelvis and for developing muscle memory for the pedaling skills.

### Loves Gathering and Collecting Objects

**Sensory Explanation:** This is a very common sensory anchor for many children and can be very soothing and calming for them. It provides a sense of control within the environment, whereas the rest of the world may be a very unpredictable, scary, and uncomfortable place. This also serves as a type of visual input that is regulating. It is very common for the child to want to carry one of these objects everywhere.

### Ideas to Help!

- No harm done with this sensory signal! Please respect this as a sensory need and a very important regulator for the nervous system. Be patient and allow for the child to pick up yet one more rock.
- Realize that the object/collectible truly has significant meaning to the child; try not to minimize it just because it lacks importance to you.
- Set aside time and play which nurtures this gathering and collecting, and find ways to organize and store the items in a safe place. When you show interest and respect in the collecting, it helps the child with self-confidence and sense of self.

## Stairs and/or Uneven Surfaces Cause Fear or Avoidance

**Sensory Explanation:** This can be explained by decreased registration of proprioceptive input and possibly muscle control and motor planning of the lower body. This in turn creates difficulty with body awareness and body in space. If the child is not comfortable with where the body is in space, stairs and uneven surfaces can be a scary thing. This can also be caused by various neuromuscular conditions/deficits and needs to be assessed/ruled out by an OT or PT.

### Ideas to Help!

- Encourage heavy/hard work activities.
- Have the child wear compression clothing, weighted belt, or weighted shoe pockets.
- Practice walking up and down small hills, going backwards and forwards.
- Encourage jumping on a trampoline, BOSU® ball, or hippity hop ball.
- Provide deep pressure touch in regular doses.
- Encourage child to climb slides at the park.
- Encourage deep breathing during new and challenging activities.

## In Constant Motion/Does Not Sit Still

**Sensory Explanation:** Likely under-registration of vestibular input is present. The brain requires an adequate amount of vestibular input to regulate and maintain a ready state to function on a daily basis. If a child is not registering or detecting the input, he/she will likely seek it out on a constant basis. The brain needs vestibular nutrition to function, and if the message is getting lost on the way, the child will crave it and be constantly hungry for it.

### Ideas to Help!

- Provide an indoor swing such as the Ikea® Ekorre swing or a hammock swing.
- Encourage the use of a hippity hop ball or BOSU® ball.
- Encourage the use of a large therapy ball for indoor use.
- Encourage inverting the head frequently.
- Encourage headstands, wheelbarrow walking, and tumbling.
- Encourage jumping from BOSU® ball to pillow cave.
- Provide opportunities for swimming and playing on swings, slides, and scooter boards.
- Encourage swinging in quick changing planes of movement and diagonal planes.
- Allow for rotational swinging, primarily in prone, 10 revolutions, one per second, then switch to the other direction.

### Very Rigid with Color Preference

**Sensory Explanation:** Children with sensory differences often crave sameness within their environment, and this can sometimes spill over into color choices and preferences. If the child is very visually driven and regulates via visual input, then this is even more likely. Once a color preference is established, the brain may find it to be very soothing and calming.

### Ideas to Help!

- Respect this as a sensory need and try not to minimize it.
- If possible, allow for the color preference…no harm done.
- Encourage other types of regulating input via the power sensations to help with overall self-regulation.
- Encourage deep breathing.
- Offer other types of visually rewarding and soothing input such as looking at an aquarium or lava lamp, etc.

### Loves to Make Mouth Noises, Such as Humming, Clicking

**Sensory Explanation:** This is a common sensory anchor and can assist in self-regulation for a child. The auditory input can be soothing and calming, as well as the proprioception and tactile input it provides to the jaw, mouth, and throat.

### Ideas to Help!

- Allow for the child to do this during times when it is not disruptive to others.
- Take note if this occurs at certain times…Is it a new and stressful situation? Or when the child is bored and required to sit? In the car?
- Provide a vibrating toothbrush or other vibrating oral sensory tool.
- Provide an MP3 player with their favorite songs and calming music.
- If the child is doing this to tune out auditory distractions, encourage the use of earplugs or noise cancelling headphones and decrease the auditory distractions when possible.
- Encourage the bubble mountain experience.

### Craves Fast, Spinning, or Intense Movement

**Sensory Explanation:** This is likely due to under-registration of vestibular input, including rotary input. The brain requires an adequate amount of vestibular input to regulate and maintain a ready state to function on a daily basis. If children are not registering or detecting the input, they will likely seek it out in powerful ways so that their brain actually feels it.

**Ideas to Help!**

- Discourage children from intense, lengthy spinning, even if they say they like it. This is very disorganizing to the brain.
- Allow spinning in small doses…one revolution per second, 10 times one way, and then 10 times the other way.
- Encourage swinging activities in various positions (sitting, on tummy, reclined), in different planes of movement, and with frequent stops and bumps.
- Encourage inverting the head often.
- Encourage jumping from BOSU® ball or mini trampoline to pillow cave.
- Encourage rolling down hills or doing somersaults.

### Spins Indefinitely and Does Not Get Dizzy

**Sensory Explanation:** This is likely due to under registration of vestibular input, primarily rotary input. The brain requires an adequate amount of vestibular input to regulate and maintain a ready state to function on a daily basis. If children are not registering or detecting the input, they will likely seek it out in powerful ways so their brain feels it. Likely the child has an under-responsive post-rotary nystagmus (PRN), in which his/her brain does not detect the rotary input; therefore, the child does not get dizzy.

**Ideas to Help!**

- Discourage children from intense, lengthy spinning, even if they say they like it. This is very disorganizing to the brain.
- Allow spinning in small doses…one revolution per second, 10 times one way, and then 10 times the other way.
- Encourage swinging activities in various positions (sitting, on tummy, reclined), and in different planes of movement.
- Encourage inverting the head regularly. Use a therapy ball.
- Encourage hanging upside down from monkey bars.
- Encourage jumping from BOSU® ball or mini trampoline to soft landing pad.
- Encourage jumping on a hippity hop ball.

### Hand Flapping

**Sensory Explanation:** This sensory signal is often misunderstood. Flapping of the hands is often a sensory anchor, which is calming and regulating to the brain. Doing this provides proprioception to the arms and hands, which is typically organizing and soothing for the nervous system. Take note if your child does this more often in new and unfamiliar settings or in challenging multi-sensory situations.

### Ideas to Help!

- It's okay to let 'em do it...and be sure to educate those around you about this sensory need. Also provide an explanation so that the child is respected for this.
- Hand flapping is really no different than someone who bites their nails, although for some reason our society accepts that as okay vs. hand flapping.
- Encourage regular doses of joint compression and joint traction via activities such as wheelbarrow walking, hanging from a bar, etc.
- Provide Thera-Putty™, Playdoh®, clay, and/or fidget toys.
- Provide regular doses of deep pressure touch to the arms and hands.
- Try Theraband® activities.
- Compression clothing for the upper body may help.

### Never Just Walks...Always Hopping, Skipping, Stomping

**Sensory Explanation:** Hopping, skipping, and stomping provide a greater amount of proprioceptive and vestibular input than simply walking. When children have difficulty self-regulating, they often require and seek out proprioceptive and/or vestibular input. This may be observed even more frequently in stressful or new situations or during a transition from one activity to another.

### Ideas to Help!

- Let the child hop, skip, and stomp instead of walking! As long as it is not disruptive or compromising safety, allowing the child to get a dose of much needed proprioception will be beneficial to his/her brain.
- Encourage frequent heavy/hard work activities.
- Have the child wear compression clothing or a Bear Hug™ compression vest.
- Provide a Camelbak® water backpack or weighted belt.
- Encourage the use of a BOSU® ball, trampoline, or hippity hop ball.
- Provide opportunities for climbing slides at the park.
- Encourage jumping down from a safe height onto both feet.

## Frequent Squinting or Fading Eye Movements

**Sensory Explanation:** Squinting and fading eye movements create unique and constantly changing visual input…this often feels good to the nervous system. This can also be done for the opposite reason, which is to filter out overwhelming visual input…if indeed the child over-registers visual input. This is also often a coping mechanism to avoid eye contact.

### Ideas to Help!

- In challenging and over-stimulating settings, encourage the use of sunglasses or floppy hat.
- Do not insist on eye contact. This must be respected as a sensory signal.
- Do not stop the child from the squinting or fading eye movements. Respect it as a sensory signal.
- Be sure visual acuity and visual perceptual concerns have been ruled out.
- Provide other visually soothing tools.
- Since this likely ties in to self-regulation, be sure to encourage regular doses of input throughout the day via the power sensations.
- Limit screen time to no more than a total of two hours per day.

## Rocks Body, Shakes Leg, or Moves Head While Sitting

**Sensory Explanation:** All three of these movements are stimulating the vestibular system, which in turn promotes attention to task, alertness, and overall self-regulation. Often these are noticed when a child is required to sit still for a period of time or in times of stress, sensory overload, or sensory dysregulation.

### Ideas to Help!

- Use a ball chair or T-stool instead of a regular seat.
- Use Thera-Band® around legs of a regular chair to provide resistance and movement for the lower body.
- Provide frequent movement breaks including heavy/hard work.
- Encourage the use of a hippity hop ball or BOSU® ball.
- Provide an indoor hammock or Ikea® swing.
- Provide a fidget toy/object or oral sensory tool such as chewing gum.
- If noted during sensory overload or multi-sensory settings, decrease the amount of sensory input overall.

### Limp/Floppy Body

**Sensory Explanation:** This is likely due to under-registration of proprioceptive feedback from the muscles and joints, as well as a sluggish vestibular system which has difficulty detecting changes in posture or position in space. This can also be related to other neuromuscular conditions, so be sure that these have been ruled out.

### Ideas to Help!

- Provide vertical vestibular input such as a trampoline, hippity hop ball, BOSU® ball, or sitting/bouncing on a therapy ball.
- Have the child wear full body compression clothing.
- Provide frequent doses of full body deep pressure touch.
- Encourage heavy/hard work activities.
- Encourage swinging in different planes.
- Give lots of bear hugs.
- Set up obstacle courses.
- Provide opportunities for jumping and landing on a soft surface such as a pillow cave.

### Always Slams Doors and Cabinets

**Sensory Explanation:** Slamming doors and cabinets provides proprioceptive input to the arms. This can be very organizing and regulating for the nervous system. It may also meet an auditory need for those who seek out sound and under-register auditory input.

### Ideas to Help!

- Encourage other types of proprioception for the arms and hands such as joint traction and joint compression via hanging from a bar, wheelbarrow walking, etc.
- Provide regular doses of deep pressure touch to the arms and hands.
- Encourage other productive, meaningful activities which involve proprioception to the arms, such as hammer type toys, racquet ball, T-ball, etc.
- Encourage activities using Theraband® and Theratubing®.
- Encourage musical instruments such as drums or a keyboard/piano.
- Play catch using a weighted medicine ball.

### Presses Hands and Feet Against Other People

**Sensory Explanation:** When children do this, they are receiving proprioceptive input and deep pressure touch, both which are very calming and regulating to the nervous system. It is also a way to feel where their body is in space and provides feedback for body awareness.

### Ideas to Help!

- This really is good for the child. Let 'em do it, and respect it as a sensory signal and a sensory need.
- In return, provide deep pressure touch while sitting with the child.
- Vibrating toys and a vibrating pillow may be helpful.
- Try compression clothing, a weighted blanket, or weighted lap pad.
- Offer a squish box or a pillow cave.
- Offer activities for joint compression and joint traction to the arms and legs.
- If you have a dog, encourage the dog to lay over the child.
- Play the steam roller game!
- Try full body massage using a weighted ball.
- Roll a therapy ball firmly over the child while he/she is lying on the floor.

### Bugs Cause Fear

**Sensory Explanation:** This is likely related to an over-responsive tactile system as well as difficulty with self-regulation. When the nervous system is on the brink of fight or flight, unexpected light touch can be overwhelming. Also, due to the fact the bugs can unexpectedly bite, tickle, or cause a pain response in an unpredictable fashion, one might expect a fearful response. This can also be related to sensory modulation difficulties.

### Ideas to Help!

- Respect this fear as real.
- Encourage deep breathing during a bug encounter.
- Allow the child to remove him/herself briefly from the environment to come back to ready state.
- Talking the child through the situation will likely not help since he/she is in fight or flight mode.
- When the child is in a ready state and regulated state of mind, read books about bugs. Also, go outside to observe non-threatening bugs, such as ladybugs and butterflies.
- Encourage tactile based play with different textures, both wet and dry, with full body play if possible.

### Bangs Head on Walls or Other Objects

**Sensory Explanation:** Banging one's head provides proprioception to the joints of the neck. This obviously is not a good idea since it can be harmful to the brain if done too often or too hard. It is indeed a powerful way for a child to feel proprioception, which in turn helps the child with self-regulation. This movement of the head also provides vestibular input, which can be organizing and regulating.

**Ideas to Help!**

- Safety first. If your child does this on a regular basis, a soft helmet is strongly recommended.
- Provide frequent regular doses of deep pressure touch to the head.
- Encourage inverting the head.
- Encourage head stands with help, if needed.
- Provide an indoor swing for regular doses of movement.
- Try a rocking chair.
- Encourage hippity hop ball or therapy ball activities.
- Try a BOSU® ball or mini-trampoline.

### Constantly Tapping Objects or Toys

**Sensory Explanation:** Tapping things provides proprioceptive input to the arms and hands as well as auditory input (often in rhythmical fashion), both of which may serve as a sensory anchor for the child and may be calming and regulating for the nervous system.

**Ideas to Help!**

- It's okay to let 'em do it if it is not distracting others. Realize that this is meeting a sensory need for the brain and nervous system.
- Provide fidget toys, clay, or Theraputty™.
- Try Theraband® or Theratubing® exercises.
- Encourage the use of toys which have levers and moveable parts to help meet this need.
- Encourage musical instruments such as drums or a keyboard/piano.
- Engage in clapping games and songs.
- Play games using a metronome.

## Swimming Is Avoided or Causes Fear

**Sensory Explanation:** Two factors may be involved with the fear of swimming. Under-registration of proprioception and a decreased sense of body awareness and body in space can be a major component, as well as tactile defensiveness. Splashing water can be very painful or uncomfortable to a child with over-responsive tactile receptors, especially involving the face. Also, water getting in the ears involves the tactile system.

### Ideas to Help!

- Try goggles or a mask and swimmers' earplugs.
- Prior to swimming, a quick trip to the park for 10-15 minutes of heavy/hard work play and movement can prepare the body and nervous system.
- A tight wetsuit can help with proprioceptive feedback and body awareness.
- Do not force the issue of swimming until the child is ready, as a forced approach will very likely set the child back.
- Encourage deep breathing to offset the fight or flight response.

## Always Tapping Hands or Feet

**Sensory Explanation:** Tapping of the hands or feet or both provides proprioceptive input to the arms and/or legs, and when it involves tapping of the feet, the vestibular system is activated as well. These may serve as a sensory anchor for the child and can be calming and regulating for the nervous system. A child will also tend to do this as a way to self-regulate and maintain ready state to focus and attend to a task.

### Ideas to Help!

- For homework or at school, allow for the use of a ball chair.
- Wrap Theraband® around the legs of the chair.
- Try a fidget toy.
- Offer a vibrating toy or pillow.
- Try an oral sensory tool to help regulate and attend.
- Have the child engage in 15 minutes of proprioceptive and vestibular play prior to tasks in which sitting is required.
- Allow the child to stand to do schoolwork, or stand on a balance board or BOSU® ball.

### Loves to Hang Upside Down Off of Things

**Sensory Explanation:** Inverting the head is EXCELLENT for the brain and nervous system and promotes self-regulation. It can be alerting or calming, depending on the state of regulation at any given moment. A child who tends to do this often under-registers vestibular input and this is a powerful way to actually feel it. The child may also struggle with self-regulation or sensory modulation, and this is a go-to technique that helps him/her feel better. Hanging upside down also provides proprioception and traction to the spine, both of which are organizing and calming for the brain.

### Ideas to Help!

- Encourage inverting the head as often as the child desires!
- Also encourage other types of vestibular input such as an indoor swing, BOSU® ball, hippity hop, etc.
- Provide regular doses of deep pressure touch.
- Encourage joint compression and joint traction activities.
- Since your child seems to seek this out, use it as a sensory strategy at times of sensory overload.
- Always have a sensory retreat available for free choice use.
- Offer regular doses of heavy/hard work (proprioception).

### Loud or Unexpected Sounds Are Startling or Cause Fear
### (Automatic hand dryer, toilet flushing, dog barking, vacuum cleaner, blender)

**Sensory Explanation:** This is likely related to an auditory system that over-registers input as well as possible difficulty with self-regulation and sensory modulation. When the nervous system is on the brink of fight or flight, unexpected, loud sounds can be overwhelming. A child who has difficulties with auditory processing may be unable to filter out irrelevant sounds and frequencies such as high pitch and deep tones.

### Ideas to Help!

- When possible, warn the child of loud upcoming sounds such as the blender or vacuum. Let the child leave the room or use headphones, earplugs, or simply cover the ears.
- Be sure noise cancelling headphones or earplugs are readily available, for home and community.
- Being aware of automatic dryers or toilets is essential. Shield the sensor when possible.
- Encourage movement activities, as vestibular input helps with auditory processing.
- Encourage deep breathing.
- Provide regular doses of full body deep pressure touch.

### Frequently Rubs Ears and Head

**Sensory Explanation:** This may be explained in a few different ways. If the child is non-verbal, this may be an indicator of a headache or ear infection, so be sure that these medical reasons are ruled out. From a sensory standpoint, doing this provides proprioception and deep pressure touch, as well as unique auditory input when done to the ears. This may also be an indicator of sensory overload from sound, and may also be due to generalized sensory overload.

### Ideas to Help!

- Provide regular doses of deep pressure touch to the head, ears, and cheeks.
- Provide head compressions via headstands or gentle pressure to the top of the head.
- Provide ear plugs, noise cancelling headphones, and sunglasses or a floppy hat if sensory overload and sensitivity seems to be the trigger.
- Invert the head.
- Try a vibrating pillow.
- Provide an oral sensory tool, including one that vibrates.
- Try a bubble mountain.

### Distracted by or Fearful of Loud Outdoor Sounds (Garbage Truck, Lawn Mower, Sirens)

**Sensory Explanation:** This is likely related to an over-responsive auditory system as well as difficulty with self-regulation. When the nervous system is on the brink of fight or flight, unexpected loud sounds can be overwhelming. A child who has difficulties with auditory processing is likely unable to filter out irrelevant sounds and frequencies, such as high pitched sounds, deep tones, and everything in between.

### Ideas to Help!

- For sounds which can be predicted, warn the child so he/she can be prepared.
- Noise cancelling headphones, earplugs, or MP3 can be very helpful during these situations.
- Encourage movement activities, as vestibular input helps with auditory processing.
- Encourage deep breathing.
- Offer a sensory retreat to help regulate after this type of sensory experience.
- Provide full body deep pressure touch, including to the head.

### Thumb Sucking

**Sensory Explanation:** Thumb sucking is a very primitive way to self-regulate for infants via oral sensory input and proprioception. It can help the child soothe, calm, tolerate the world around them, and avoid sensory overload. Many children with sensory differences suck their thumbs well past 5 years old…for the exact same reasons as when they were infants, but the difference is that now they are interacting and exploring the world on their own, which can be even more challenging. You will likely observe your child thumb sucking in challenging, overwhelming, or new situations…as well as a way to soothe, possibly to fall asleep.

### Ideas to Help!

- Transition slowly to other oral sensory tools such as an ARK Grabber® or Camelbak® water bottle.
- Offer bubble mountain on a daily basis.
- Determine other possible triggers of sensory overload such as sound, smells, etc., and offer tools for defensiveness as appropriate.
- Provide a sensory retreat.
- Offer a squish box.
- Encourage deep breathing on a regular basis.
- Provide regular doses of proprioception throughout the day.
- Provide full body deep pressure touch throughout the day.

### Bites Fingernails

**Sensory Explanation:** Biting fingernails provides proprioceptive input to the jaw joints as well as oral sensory input to the mouth and tactile input to the fingers. This often serves as a sensory anchor for the child, and also may be a tool to assist with maintaining ready state, attention to task, or self-regulation. This quite often becomes a habit as well, due to the engram created in the brain, which makes it very difficult to stop.

### Ideas to Help!

- Encourage the use of an oral sensory tool such as a Camelbak® water bottle or Chewelry®.
- Offer a fidget toy.
- Provide regular doses of deep pressure touch to the hands and fingers.
- Try Theraputty™, clay, and Play-doh®.
- Offer bubble mountain and other resistive blowing activities such as a harmonica or recorder.
- Take note of when this is done most often. If during schoolwork, try other sensory tools such as a ball chair. If in the car, be sure to have sensory tools available to replace.

## Asks Others to Stop Talking or Laughing

**Sensory Explanation:** This is likely due to a difficulty in auditory processing and auditory defensiveness. This can also be related to sensory modulation and overall self-regulation. If the child is on the brink of fight or flight and sensory overload on a regular basis, then talking and laughing can be the trigger to send the nervous system over the edge. Talking and laughing involve various frequencies in sound and pitch and tone changes. This can be overwhelming and uncomfortable to the child, especially when there are multiple people talking.

### Ideas to Help!

- Be aware and respectful of this, and let the child leave the room if possible when there is too much talking and laughing going on.
- Provide noise cancelling headphones or earplugs.
- Provide an MP3 player.
- Encourage movement activities, as vestibular input helps with auditory processing.
- Provide a sensory retreat.
- If the child cannot be removed from the environment, provide a bear hug or other deep pressure touch to assist with self-regulation.
- Allow for the use of a floppy hat, fisherman's hat, or sunglasses to help decrease overall sensory input.
- Do not insist on eye contact in social situations; let this happen naturally.
- Refrain from drawing attention to the child in a social setting.

## Always Carries a Special Object Everywhere They Go

**Sensory Explanation:** This is a very common sensory anchor for many children, and can be soothing and calming for them. It provides a sense of control within the environment, whereas the rest of the world can be a very unpredictable, scary, and uncomfortable place. This can also provide a comforting form of tactile input to the hands. It is quite common for the child to carry an object everywhere.

### Ideas to Help!

- It's okay, let 'em do it! Respect it as a sensory need that assists with self-regulation.
- Try various fidget toys as alternatives.
- Address overall self-regulation via regular doses of proprioception and vestibular input throughout the day.
- If the preferred object is just too big (like a two foot stick), then try to encourage replacing the object with something smaller and meaningful, such as a rough or smooth stone. Let the child choose the replacement, of course.

## Runs Away or Covers Ears in Response to Loud or Unexpected Sounds

**Sensory Explanation:** This is likely related to auditory defensiveness where the brain over-registers sound. This can also be due to difficulties with self-regulation and sensory modulation. When the nervous system is on the brink of fight or flight, unexpected, loud sounds can be overwhelming and be the trigger which sends the nervous system in to sensory overload. A child who has difficulties with auditory processing is likely unable to filter out irrelevant sounds and frequencies such as high pitch and deep tones. When the auditory system over-registers auditory input, sounds are that much louder to the child.

### Ideas to Help!

- Let the child leave the room or use noise cancelling headphones, earplugs, or simply cover ears.
- Be sure noise cancelling headphones or earplugs are readily available, for home and community. It's a good idea to have two sets, one kept in the car.
- Encourage movement activities, as vestibular input helps with auditory processing.
- Encourage deep breathing.
- Provide a sensory retreat, especially when sensory overload is noted.
- Encourage the regular use of a squish box or pillow cave.
- Provide regular daily doses of proprioception to assist with self-regulation.

## Stranger Anxiety Over Age 2

**Sensory Explanation:** This is very common for children who struggle with anxiety. Anxiety in itself is often a side effect of sensory processing difficulties, especially for those who have sensory defensiveness. This is also common for children who struggle with social interaction. Children with sensory differences prefer sameness, routine, predictability…all of which are the opposite of meeting or interacting with a stranger.

### Ideas to Help!

- Respect this as a real sensory challenge; please try not to minimize it.
- Talking the child through it or justifying that it will be okay is likely not going to work.
- The nervous system is likely in a state of fight or flight or on the brink of it…address this as you would a fight or flight episode.
- A bear hug and deep pressure touch, or holding the child close without saying a word is the best approach. Let the child interact and engage within the environment on his/her own terms when ready.
- Allow for the use of a floppy hat or sunglasses or a hood to help decrease the sensory input overall.
- Let the "stranger" know that it is best to wait for the child to be ready to interact rather than forcing the issue.

## Often Makes Snorting Sounds

**Sensory Explanation:** Making nasal type sounds provides auditory input as well as proprioception to the oral structures. This also provides a form of tactile input and vibration to the ears/head/throat. This may be soothing and regulating for the child and may also serve as a sensory anchor, especially when done in a certain pattern or rhythm.

### Ideas to Help!

- Encourage the use of an oral sensory tool, especially one with vibration.
- Offer bubble mountain on a regular basis.
- Try musical instruments involving respiration such as a harmonica or recorder.
- Offer a vibrating toy or pillow.
- Encourage deep breathing.
- Play metronome games and involve fun mouth sounds.
- Try dancing, clapping, tapping, or snapping games and songs.

## T.V. or Music Must Be Excessively Loud

**Sensory Explanation:** The child's auditory system may be under-registering input. Therefore, to the child, loud music or T.V. is possibly soothing. Another explanation may be the opposite: the auditory system is over-registering, and the child may not be able to filter out irrelevant sounds. So the louder the music or T.V., the easier it is to tune in . . . and tune out the other sounds.

### Ideas to Help!

- Try the use of headphones for the music or T.V. at a reasonable sound level. With the headphones the child will be able to focus on just the music or T.V.
- Encourage movement activities, as vestibular input facilitates auditory processing.
- During movement activities such as swinging, involve an auditory game or play music.
- Offer an MP3 player with instrumental music.
- Decrease the other background noise within the room when watching T.V.
- Have the child sit on a ball chair or hippity hop ball while watching T.V.
- Encourage dancing while listening to music. This will also assist with auditory processing.

### Always Rocking or Tilting Chair

**Sensory Explanation:** Doing this activates the vestibular system, which is often needed to attend to task, maintain a ready state for learning, or for basic self-regulation. Children who under-register vestibular input tend to need to move to learn and will wiggle in any way they can while seated. Rocking or tilting the chair is just one more way to seek movement.

**Ideas to Help!**

- Switch out the regular chair for a ball chair or hippity hop ball at school and at home at a desk.
- Try Theraband® wrapped around the legs of the chair.
- Encourage sitting on a vibrating pillow or place it under the feet.
- An oral sensory tool may be helpful.
- Explore fidget toy options.
- Encourage regular doses of vestibular input during the day, especially prior to sit down tasks.
- Encourage at least 15 minutes of movement and proprioception prior to being seated.
- Instead of sitting for schoolwork or homework, let the child stand or lay on the floor on their tummy.
- Try doing schoolwork on a vertical surface such as an easel, chalkboard or dry erase board; this could also be done with a BOSU® ball or use of a balance board.

### Visual Stimuli in the Room is Distracting

**Sensory Explanation:** Visual processing is often overlooked or taken for granted. A child who has difficulty with visual processing may have a very hard time sorting out all of the visual input in any given setting. This can particularly be a problem at school, as the walls and room are often overloaded with visual stimuli (display boards, posters, shelves with many items, things hanging from the ceiling, fluorescent lighting, etc.).

**Ideas to Help!**

- Be hyper-aware of the visual stimuli in the child's environment. Organization is the key, and clutter needs to be removed to help the child self-regulate.
- When outdoors or in busy environments, let the child wear a floppy hat, fisherman type hat, or sunglasses to cut down on visual stimuli.
- Eliminate fluorescent lighting if possible. Natural light is best.
- Keep a tidy home and stay organized.

### Waves Arms on a Regular Basis

**Sensory Explanation:** Waving arms provides proprioceptive input to the arms, and depending on the intensity, possibly vestibular input. This can be a method of self-regulating or serve as a sensory anchor, particularly in challenging settings or to avoid sensory overload and/or fight or flight.

### Ideas to Help!

- Respect this as a means to help self-regulate, and as long is the child is not whacking someone when waving the arms, let 'em do it.
- Long sleeved compression clothing for the upper body may help.
- Encourage hanging from bars.
- Install a trapeze swing at home or a door frame pull-up bar to hang from for joint traction.
- Try deep pressure touch to the child's arms on a regular basis.
- Vibration to the child's arms and hands may be helpful.
- Try Theraband® exercises for the arms, and also using the Theraband® wrapped over the shoulders.
- If arm waving seems to only occur in new and/or multi-sensory settings, establish the triggers and offer tools for defensiveness as needed.

### Bath Time is Difficult

**Sensory Explanation:** If a child is resisting bath time, there is most likely one or more sensory triggers causing the experience to be uncomfortable for the nervous system. There are so many components involved during a bath, so be sure to assess each aspect as a possible trigger.

### Ideas to Help!

- If your child is sensitive to sound, bathrooms often have an echo…Place numerous bathmats or rugs on the floor to help with this. The bathmats and rugs will also help the tactile system and the unexpected change of texture and temperature for little bare feet.
- You may want to have the child use swimmer's earplugs and/or goggles or a swimmer's face mask to help avoid the unexpected tactile input from the water droplets.
- Determine if the smells of the soaps are bothersome. Natural soaps and shampoos are strongly encouraged.
- Make sure bath time is fun and not rushed; let it be a time to relax and enjoy the water.
- Encourage as much independence as possible during bathing, instead of the rushed scrub down. Teach the child how to bathe.
- Play relaxing, instrumental music during bath time to promote self-regulation.
- Begin bath time with bubble mountain in the bath tub!
- Use a very soft wash cloth if tactile defensiveness is an issue.

## Lines Are Followed with Eyes, Such as Countertops, Edges of Toys, Books

**Sensory Explanation:** Visual input can be very organizing and regulating for the brain, especially to a child who has difficulty with self-regulation. This sensory signal is also considered a sensory anchor which can be a sign that the child is having a difficult time regulating.

### Ideas to Help!

- Use this sensory signal as an indicator that the child needs help regulating. Encourage heavy/hard work or movement play.
- Respect this as a sensory anchor. Do not treat this as a behavior by making the child stop.
- Be sure the visual surroundings overall are not overwhelming or cluttered.
- Provide other visually soothing activities such as watching fish in an aquarium, watching marbles go through a maze or possibly a labyrinth maze.
- Encourage the use of a pillow cave or a body sock with a flashlight inside for visual input.

## Constant Pen Clicking

**Sensory Explanation:** Clicking of a pen provides tactile and proprioceptive feedback to the hand and fingers, as well as auditory input. Often the pen clicking will be done in a pattern or rhythmical fashion. All of these types of input combined can be very soothing and regulating for the nervous system. This may also serve as a sensory anchor for the child. Believe it or not, simply clicking the pen can help the brain in regard to learning and attention.

### Ideas to Help!

- Respect this as a sensory signal and allow for the pen clicking when it is not disturbing others.
- When it's necessary to replace this with something non-distracting, a fidget toy would be a great alternative.
- Encourage the use of a ball chair for homework or at school instead of a regular chair.
- Have the child try lying on their tummy to do school work or standing and working on a vertical surface such as an easel.
- Try having the child use an MP3 player and ear buds listening to instrumental music while doing school work.
- Encourage regular movement breaks during school work.

## Gets Easily Frustrated

**Sensory Explanation:** This is very common for our children with sensory differences, especially those children who struggle with sensory modulation and self-regulation. When a child's nervous system is spending a significant amount of time trying to regulate and maintain a ready state in order to interact within the environment, process and adapt sensory input, and develop and learn, challenging tasks can send the brain into overload and possibly fight or flight. Sometimes the trigger for frustration is one small bit of sensory input . . . input that would not typically cause frustration...yet at the brink of sensory overload, almost all input is a threat.

### Ideas to Help!

- Respect this signal as a sign of dysregulation, not a behavior.
- Refrain from talking the child through the situation. The brain is not in a cortical level of processing.
- Take a break, involving movement or heavy/hard work play, then return to the previous task.
- Allow the child to take a break in a quiet, calm, possibly dark place.
- Provide a sensory retreat such as a pillow cave or play tent.
- Encourage deep breathing.
- Encourage resistive blowing, such as a bubble mountain.
- Assess the situation for specific sensory triggers, such as sound, and provide tools for defensiveness.

## Temperature in Bath Must be "Just Right"

**Sensory Explanation:** The tactile system (the pain and temperature pathway) is responsible for processing the feeling of something being hot or cold. Children who over-register tactile input may also over-register temperature, where something that is cool may feel bitter cold, or something warm my feel scalding hot.

### Ideas to Help!

- Please be patient and take the time to achieve the "just right" temperature. Let your child help by testing the water with one finger if they so desire.
- Encourage full body messy play on a regular basis to help with overall tactile processing.
- Regular and frequent tactile play in all types of mediums will also help with overall tactile processing.
- Provide daily doses of deep pressure touch.
- Encourage water play in the sink and outdoors to increase the number of positive experiences involving water.

### Mood Changes Quickly and Unexpectedly

**Sensory Explanation:** Mood is controlled by the area in the brain responsible for self-regulation. If self-regulating is a challenge for the child, then quick shifts in mood are likely to occur without warning or reason. Shifts in mood may also be triggered by sensory overload and/or fight or flight. This is also very common for children who struggle with sensory modulation.

**Ideas to Help!**

- Respect this signal as a sign of dysregulation, not a behavior.
- Refrain from talking the child through the situation. The brain is not in a cortical level of processing.
- Encourage movement or heavy/hard work play.
- Allow the child to take a break in a quiet, calm, possibly dark place.
- Provide a sensory retreat, such as a pillow cave or play tent.
- Provide deep pressure touch, bear hugs, or weighted blanket.
- Encourage deep breathing.
- Bubble mountain is a great activity for self-regulation.
- A squish box may be helpful.
- Provide frequent daily doses of vertical vestibular input.

### Does Not Like Kisses, Wipes Them Off

**Sensory Explanation:** Kisses are often not well tolerated since there is unexpected and variable tactile input. Soft kisses activate the light touch receptors and firm kisses activate deep pressure touch receptors. And then you have the variable of a wet or dry kiss. Children who struggle with tactile defensiveness most likely will not like being kissed. The facial tactile receptors can be even more challenging. Think of being kissed on the back of your hand versus on the cheek, it is a whole different sensation.

**Ideas to Help!**

- A big bear hug is a great alternative to a kiss.
- If a kiss is irresistible, then make sure it is a firm, dry kiss. And please give the child warning.
- Another great alternative for affection is to place your cheek firmly against the child's cheek, and move your jaw up and down. Then have the child do it back to you.
- Regular doses of deep pressure touch to the head and the face can be helpful for tactile processing.

### Does Not Like to Hold Hands

**Sensory Explanation:** There can be a couple of different sensory explanations for this one. If the child struggles with tactile defensiveness, than this can truly be uncomfortable to the hand. Another explanation can be if the child is a sensory seeker and under-registers sensory input overall. In this case, the urge to run and jump and explore is just way too appealing!

**Ideas to Help!**

- If tactile defensiveness is the issue, the wearing of rings can be the trigger for the child not wanting to hold hands. Take your rings off while holding hands.
- Firmly grip the child's full hand and provide uniform, deep pressure touch while holding hands.
- It may also be helpful for the child to wear tight fitting gloves while holding hands to decrease the tactile input, and also to provide some compression from the gloves.
- If your child is a seeker and simply wants to be free for the sensory input, give the child the opportunity for movement for at least 15 minutes prior to needing to hold hands for an extended period of time.
- You could also try making the holding of hands fun by marching together, hopping, skipping, etc.

### Going to Sleep, Staying Asleep, or Waking Up in the Morning Is Difficult

**Sensory Explanation:** The sleep/wake cycle and ability to transition to and from sleep is controlled by the area of the brain which facilitates self-regulation. Children who have a difficult time with self-regulation often have difficulty with sleep patterns. Children who under-register sensory input also tend to have a hard time with sleep, since the body is constantly craving and needing sensory input.

**Ideas to Help!**

- Proprioception is the key to going to sleep, staying asleep, and in turn… a restful night's sleep.
- Provide a weighted blanket or heavy quilt folded up.
- Have the child wear compression clothing or tight, full length cotton pajamas.
- Provide a vibrating pillow.
- Provide a Lycra™ compression sheet as an alternative to a weighted blanket which may be too warm for some children.
- Provide full body deep pressure touch right before bed.
- Provide an oral sensory tool.
- Let the child sleep in the pillow cave or a cozy pillow-filled spot on the bed.
- Allow the child to sleep in a sensory retreat.
- Play soft, soothing instrumental music or white noise.
- Provide a Slumber Bear or other heartbeat stuffed animal.
- Provide at least 15 minutes of calming, rhythmical swinging prior to bedtime; preferably in a hammock swing or cuddle swing.
- It is strongly encouraged not to allow your child to engage in any screen time at least one hour prior to bedtime; reading is a better option to promote sleep.
- If your child wants a snack prior to bedtime, be sure it is high in protein rather than sugar and carbs.

### Flushing of Face, Hives, Random Fever, or Nausea

**Sensory Explanation:** Sensory overload can present itself in many ways, including systemic reactions such as those listed above. Of course, there are many other medical explanations and reasons which should absolutely be ruled out, but when any of the above symptoms seem to happen at times of sensory stress or in a challenging sensory environment, this is an explanation to consider. This is particularly an issue with vestibular input.

**Ideas to Help!**

- Play close attention to these warning signs when your child is engaged in a new sensory activity, especially those involving movement.
- Stop a sensory activity immediately of you notice any of these signs.
- Offer a sensory retreat to help recover from the sensory overload.
- Encourage deep breathing and possibly an oral sensory tool to help recover.
- A squish box or a body sock is a great tool to use as well.
- Full body deep pressure touch may be helpful.

### Hides Under Bed, Under Table, or in Closet

**Sensory Explanation:** Cozy and dark spaces minimize auditory and visual input. Tight spaces provide proprioception to assist in self-regulation. Combine these and you have a wonderful little sensory retreat for a child in sensory overload, or a child who has realized that the calming input feels great for the nervous system.

**Ideas to Help!**

- Respect this signal as a sign that the child is likely in sensory overload or needs the input to help regulate. Allow the child to stay there until ready to come out.
- Provide a sensory retreat for regular use as an alternative.
- Provide a squish box in a nice, cozy, dark place.
- Provide a pillow cave.
- Provide a body sock or fabric tunnel.
- At school, provide a sensory retreat as an alternative to the child going under the desk.
- When auditory or visual input are the triggers, offer tools for defensiveness as a proactive strategy to avoid sensory overload or the need to retreat/hide.

## Enjoys Repetitive Play

**Sensory Explanation:** Repetitive play can be very soothing and organizing for a child with sensory processing and/or self-regulation difficulties. It gives the child a sense of sameness and predictability, which can be comforting. This may be a type of sensory anchor for the child. Repetitive play can sometimes turn into a maladaptive behavior; it then becomes very hard to redirect or stop the repetition.

### Ideas to Help!

Repetitive play in moderation is just fine, since it helps with self-regulation. If it becomes difficult to redirect or stop the repetition, it is a good idea to use the following suggestions:

- If you see a pattern or repetition beginning (such as the child going down the same slide over and over), casually redirect him/her and engage in various alternative fun activities to break the pattern.
- Encourage heavy/hard work and movement play throughout the day.
- Set a timer and give the child a 5-minute warning, following up with another engaging type of sensory play as an alternative (maybe a bubble mountain).
- Provide routine and structure in the child's daily life.
- Be sure the child is receiving daily regular doses of input via the power sensations.

## Pinches Others or Self

**Sensory Explanation:** The sensory explanation for this can be two-fold. The act of pinching provides proprioceptive input to the hand/fingers which can be soothing and regulating for the nervous system, and when the child is pinching themselves, it can serve as sensory input that they can actually feel. Children who under-register sensory input often require very intense sensory input to experience the sensation. So pinching their own skin may feel good. In turn, they do not realize that others do not experience sensation differently, therefore they may not realize it hurts someone.

### Ideas to Help!

- Encourage the use of a fidget toy as a replacement, preferably one that the child can pinch.
- Regular use of Theraputty™, clay, or Playdoh® can help meet this proprioceptive urge.
- Provide deep pressure touch to the hands and fingers throughout the day.
- A vibrating toy or handheld massager can be helpful.
- Encourage other types of heavy/hard work play for the arms and hands.
- Wheelbarrow walking may be helpful.
- Encourage push-and-pull type activities and hanging from a trapeze or playground bar.

### Refuses to Wear Clothing and Likes to Be Naked

**Sensory Explanation:** This sensory signal is most likely observed with a child who over-registers tactile input and displays tactile defensiveness. Various textures of clothing constantly shifting on the body can be very uncomfortable and even painful for the child. On the other hand, a child may like to be naked for the unique sensory experience of the air on the skin and temperature difference.

### Ideas to Help!

- Be hyper-aware of each piece of clothing, including the texture and fit of the clothes. Let your child be the gauge of comfort and preferred textures. If you find a specific type of soft pants your child likes, I would recommend buying at least 5 pairs. ☺ The child will likely want the same pants every day. . .and that is okay - it really is. ☺
- Compression clothing may be helpful.
- Try seamless socks and seamless underwear.
- Provide regular doses of full body deep pressure touch.
- Encourage full body tactile play in various mediums, especially messy play.
- Allow for no clothing time in the privacy of your home or the child's room.
- Sometimes a very soft robe is a great alternative to clothing, and the child can be covered but not required to wear clothing under the robe.

### Impulsive

**Sensory Explanation:** A child who is impulsive likely has difficulty with self-regulation and possibly under-registers sensory input. The impulsive nature is often due to sensory seeking and the overwhelming need to meet the sensory need, which overrides any cortical level of thinking or judgment. Think of it as your child being in a sensory tunnel. Another explanation involves executive functioning, and the ability to demonstrate safety awareness and judgment, which is often lacking when sensory processing difficulties are present.

### Ideas to Help!

- Safety first . . . be very aware of this impulsive nature when playing outside or around flights of stairs or other possibly dangerous situations. Keep in mind: a child who is impulsive is unlikely to respond to a verbal command when in the moment of sensory seeking. This is not intentional.
- Frequent and regular doses of movement and heavy/hard work facilitate self-regulation and can decrease impulsivity.
- Have the child wear compression clothing or Bear Hug™ compression vest.
- Invert the head regularly.
- Encourage vertical movement such as on a trampoline, hippity hop ball, or BOSU® ball.
- Limit screen time to no more than two hours per day total.
- Encourage deep breathing on a regular basis.
- Bubble mountain is a great activity to help with self-regulation.

### Touches Everything They Pass

**Sensory Explanation:** This is most common with children who under-register tactile input. The child may crave texture on a constant basis to help regulate and soothe the nervous system. When the child touches everything they pass, they experience all sorts of texture and it can also provide deep pressure touch, depending on the amount of pressure applied.

### Ideas to Help!

- Allow the child to do this if it is not causing any harm or destruction. Parents tend to automatically tell a child to stop doing this.
- Provide regular and frequent doses of deep pressure touch to the arms and hands.
- Encourage joint compression and joint traction for the arms.
- A fidget toy when you are out and about can be helpful.
- Any oral sensory tool can also help the child regulate, and can decrease the need to touch everything.
- Encourage frequent full body tactile experiences, especially messy play.
- A vibrating toy or pillow, or handheld massager can be helpful.
- Petting animals would be a great idea.
- Exploring different textures at the fabric store would be a fun sensory outing.
- Explore different textures in nature by taking daily nature walks to meet this need.

### Falls Out of Chairs Frequently

**Sensory Explanation:** This is most likely due to decreased body awareness and body in space, along with difficulty with vestibular processing (balance and posture control). It may also be due to poor muscle tone and impaired developmental reflexes. On the other hand, a sensory seeking child may do this since the sensory input of falling to the floor feels good to the nervous system.

### Ideas to Help!

- Try a weighted lap pad.
- If in a standard chair, be sure the hips and knees are at 90 degree angles, and add a stool or sturdy book under the feet for proper positioning if needed.
- Try a ball chair for those seeking input and those working on posture.
- Provide hippity hop ball and therapy ball activities on a daily basis.
- Have the child try sitting on a vibrating pillow.
- Incorporate frequent heavy/hard work activities to improve body awareness.
- For small children, Rody (a hippity-hop ride-on horse) is a great way to work on posture and balance.

### Waiting or Standing in Line is Very Difficult

**Sensory Explanation:** Standing in line or simply waiting is very challenging for all children, and for sensory seekers and those who struggle with self-regulation, this can be nearly impossible. Not only does the child not have anything to do or preoccupy themselves, they are unable to seek out input that helps the child to regulate, such as movement or proprioception. Waiting or standing in line can also be difficult due to the anticipation factor, especially when the waiting involves something fun after the wait (such as a ride at the fair). This can also be extra difficult when self-control is needed, such as in line at the grocery store, and when surrounded by candy and things to eat and touch.

### Ideas to Help!

- When out and about in the community, make sure you have a sensory survival bag with tools for defensiveness and sensory tools to help meet various sensory needs…such as a fidget toy, oral sensory tool, MP3 player, etc.
- If possible, when standing in line, provide deep pressure touch to the shoulders and arms, and gentle head compressions. Joint traction to the arms is also a good idea.
- Provide a modified bear hug when the child is standing next to you, pressing their body against yours with your arms draped over their body and provide uniform firm pressure.
- If possible, hold the child and provide deep pressure touch.
- Play "I Spy" or another guessing game to help distract the child and to keep it fun.
- If a sturdy handrail or bar is close by, let the child hang from it for joint traction.
- Hold the child and let them lean back for a dose of head inversion.

### Bathroom Urgency/Frequent Accidents

**Sensory Explanation:** The ability to know when it is time to go to the bathroom relies on the sensory feedback to the brain from the bladder or intestines. This sensory feedback is from the interoceptors in the gut. If a child under-registers sensory information, it is possible that he/she could also under-register sensory information from the gut.

### Ideas to Help!

- Respect the fact that there may indeed be a sensory explanation. Do not scold or discipline a child who truly may not be having the sensation of needing to go until it is too late.
- There could be medical reasons for this, and it is important to rule this out with your pediatrician.
- Be sure that teachers and caregivers are aware of this sensory explanation.
- Sensory processing and registration must occur in order for this to improve.
- Believe it or not, providing overall enriched sensory activities throughout the day can help in the long run. Daily frequent doses of input via the power sensations is important.
- Focus on proprioceptive activities to promote overall body awareness.
- Try not to place expectations on the child in regards to a certain age in which the child will be fully potty trained. It is not uncommon for children with sensory differences to fully potty train after age 5.
- If the accidents are occurring at night, even more developmental time may be needed, especially for boys. This is not uncommon through at least age 6.

### Shakes or Rolls Head While Seated

**Sensory Explanation:** Shaking the head provides vestibular input for the nervous system as well as a unique visual experience. A child may be doing this for one or both of these reasons. It can be a way to self-regulate or also a way to avoid sensory overload or even to help concentrate. Some children do this in a rhythmical fashion, which serves as a sensory anchor and can be soothing and regulating. When a child is seated, the vestibular system is not receiving much input, and the brain and nervous system is in need of constant and/or a greater amount of vestibular input to maintain ready state and self-regulation.

### Ideas to Help!

- Try using a ball chair or hippity hop ball instead of a regular chair or seat.
- Prior to a seated activity, have the child engage in at least 15 minutes of movement and heavy/hard work play.
- Try using a vibrating pillow for the child to sit on or to place under the feet.
- Theraband® wrapped around the legs of the chair or wrapped over the shoulders can be useful.
- Offer a fidget toy and/or an oral sensory tool to help with overall self-regulation.
- Have the child invert the head prior to activities requiring being seated.
- Use a rocking chair or office chair that swivels as an alternative.
- Encourage regular doses of vertical vestibular input via a BOSU® ball, trampoline, or a pogo stick.

### Twists, Extends, or Holds Hands Together Tightly When Challenged or Stressed

**Sensory Explanation:** Doing this activity provides proprioceptive input to the arms and hands. This can be regulating and serve as a sensory anchor. It can also be just the right type of sensory input to prevent sensory overload or fight or flight for the child.

### Ideas to Help!

- Let 'em do it. Respect this as a sensory signal, and if it feels good and helps the child regulate, why not?
- A fidget toy may be helpful.
- Encourage deep breathing during stressful or challenging scenarios.
- Be sure to use tools for defensiveness as needed.
- Provide regular and frequent doses of deep pressure touch, especially to the arms and hands.
- Provide joint compression to the arms such as wheelbarrow walking.
- Play catch with a weighted medicine ball.
- Encourage hanging from a bar or trapeze to provide joint traction.
- Provide compression clothing for the upper body.
- Provide Theraband® activities for the arms.
- Theraputty™, clay, or Playdoh® may be useful.

### Does Not Seem to Get Hungry or Eats Way Too Much or Too Quickly

**Sensory Explanation:** The ability to know when one is hungry or full relies on the sensory feedback to the brain from the stomach. This sensory feedback is from the interoceptors in the gut. If a child under-registers sensory information, it is possible that sensory information from the gut is also under-registered. This can result in not being able to detect when he/she is full, or on the other hand, may not have much of an appetite. Stuffing food in the cheeks also provides proprioceptive feedback, which may feel good to the child's nervous system.

**Ideas to Help!**

- This is another tough one…respecting the fact that there may be a sensory explanation is important.
- Help the child pace him/herself. Often the children who eat too much also eat in a sensory-seeking fashion.
- Feed in small portions and small bites, allowing second servings if needed.
- For those who don't get hungry, a movement and heavy/hard work activity prior to mealtime can be helpful.
- Frequent and daily doses of input via the power sensations are very important to improve overall sensory registration.
- Try bubble mountain prior to eating.
- For those children who seem to do this to stuff the cheeks, an oral sensory tool throughout the day is a good idea.

### Repeats Speech Sounds or Phrases

**Sensory Explanation:** Repetitive speech is quite a bit like repetitive play, except this time the auditory system is involved, as well as some proprioception through speech production. Repetitive speech seems to be very soothing and organizing for a child with sensory processing difficulties and self-regulation difficulties. This is often a sensory anchor.

**Ideas to Help!**

- Provide an oral sensory tool.
- Use an MP3 player with the child's favorite music or instrumental music.
- Encourage resistive blowing activity such as a bubble mountain.
- Encourage singing songs instead of the repetitive speech.
- Encourage movement activities involving an auditory component.
- Try using a metronome and encourage movement and clapping games along with it.
- Try bubble mountain.
- Musical instruments such as drums, harmonica, or recorder may help.

### Gets Sick or Nauseous After Swinging

**Sensory Explanation:** Swinging involves a very powerful dose of vestibular input. Children who struggle with vestibular defensiveness or sensory modulation can quickly and without warning become sick or nauseous after swinging. This can be even more likely when there are quick changes in direction or frequent starts and stops of the swing.

### Ideas to Help!

- Watch closely for any signs of distress while swinging. Even a change in facial expression may be your only warning. Other signs to watch for include flushing of the skin or eyes glazing over.
- Begin swinging in very small doses, even one minute is powerful. Also begin in one plane of movement with very little movement of the swing.
- Prior to swinging, have the child engage in proprioceptive play.
- Encourage deep breathing while swinging.
- The use of an oral sensory tool while swinging can be helpful.

### Chews on Sleeves, Hair, Fingers, Non-Food Objects

**Sensory Explanation:** Chewing on various items provides proprioception to the jaw as well as additional oral sensory input. This can assist in self-regulation, and in turn promotes attention to task and calms the nervous system in stressful situations.

### Ideas to Help!

- Provide an oral sensory tool as an alternative and be sure that it is readily available at all times (attach to child's clothing).
- Provide a Camelbak® water backpack.
- Provide a Camelbak® water bottle.
- Provide chewing gum.
- Provide chewy foods such as turkey jerky, French bread, or taffy.
- Bubble mountain is a great activity idea.
- To promote overall self-regulation, incorporate the power sensations in to the day, every day.

### Climbs in Cabinets

**Sensory Explanation:** Climbing in to a cabinet is a creative way to establish a sensory retreat. It is often a tight space, so it also requires the body to be in full flexion, and the tight space provides deep pressure touch. Not only are these two things both very regulating, but while in the cabinet, there is a decreased amount of visual and auditory input, which is often very soothing for a child.

**Ideas to Help!**

- Let 'em do it! Not only let 'em…give them their own special empty cabinet with a cozy blanket and pillow!
- A pillow cave or squish box is sure to be a hit, as well.
- Encourage activities involving full flexion while swinging or tumbling.
- If the child seems to be trying to escape light and/or sound, provide tools for defensiveness as needed.
- Provide full body deep pressure touch.
- Place other sensory tools in the cabinet to make it extra special and sensory soothing, such as a fidget toy, vibrating pillow, or oral sensory tool.

### Licks Everything, Including People and Objects

**Sensory Explanation:** A child who licks everything is likely doing this to feel safe and identify within their environment. Children who do this are often using it as a sensory anchor to help regulate. Children who are oral sensory seekers tend to do this the most, as it is the sense that they can best relate to for processing information.

**Ideas to Help!**

- Offer an oral sensory tool as an alternative, making sure it is available at all times for the child (preferably attached to the child).
- Take note of when this happens the most…is it only in new places or with certain people or during transitions? Provide tools for defensiveness if sensory overload seems to be a factor.
- Provide regular and daily doses of proprioception to help with overall self-regulation.
- A bubble mountain would be a great tool.
- Olfactory input may also help in this case; essential oils may help soothe and regulate the child.

### Bites Self or Others

**Sensory Explanation:** The act of biting provides proprioception to the jaw and tactile input to the mouth. This provides oral sensory input, which is soothing and regulating for the brain. When the child bites him/herself, this can be due to sensory under-registration. Children who under-register input tend to crave very powerful types, and biting self may actually feel good.

### Ideas to Help!

- Offer an oral sensory tool.
- Offer chewy and crunchy foods frequently.
- Encourage resistive blowing such as a bubble mountain.
- Encourage drinking pudding, yogurt, or applesauce through a straw.
- Offer smoothies on a regular basis and milkshakes occasionally.
- Use a Camelbak® water backpack.
- Use a Camelbak® water bottle.
- Take note of when this happens the most…is it during challenging situations or sensory overload? Respond accordingly with the use of tools for defensiveness or changing the environment.
- Daily doses of input via the power sensations are critical to improve sensory registration.

### Screams at Others Instead of Verbalizing

**Sensory Explanation:** Social interaction and speech/language are very high level skills, and a child who struggles with sensory processing is almost sure to have difficulty with speech/language development and social skills. This can also be a sign of sensory dysregulation or a child on the brink of fight or flight or sensory overload.

### Ideas to Help!

- Respect this as a sensory signal and do not assume behavioral or attention seeking. The child may truly not be able to control this.
- Try using a picture board, customized picture book, or communication board to assist with communication.
- Incorporate daily doses of input via the power sensations to work on overall sensory processing development.
- Encourage deep breathing on a regular basis.
- Try to refrain from too much guessing and asking the child a million questions to determine what they need or want. This will only further dysregulate the nervous system.
- If possible, provide a sensory retreat with calming tools to help in the event of sensory overload.
- Assess the situation to determine if specific sensory triggers seem to be causing this, such as too much auditory input, too many people, etc.

## Circle Time Difficulty at School

**Sensory Explanation:** Circle time is a multi-sensory experience and requires adequate sensory processing skills in order to respond in an adaptive fashion. It requires great demand for the nervous system and should not be taken lightly. Circle time not only involves the child being required to sit still; there are unpredictable bumps and brushes against the skin from others, a child talking way too loud next to them, and the demands of following instructions and possibly having attention drawn to the child during a circle time activity.

### Ideas to Help!

- Provide a squish box to be used during circle time.
- Provide a fidget toy.
- Provide a weighted blanket or lap pad.
- Provide an oral sensory tool.
- Prior to circle time have the child engage in 5-10 minutes of movement or heavy/hard work group activity.
- Provide a ball chair.
- Provide a T-stool.
- Allow child to lie on tummy.
- Use a body sock.
- Provide a vibrating pillow for the child to sit on or hold.
- If the child is defensive to touch, have that child sit on one end of the half circle, which will decrease the tactile input by 50%.
- Encourage the use of tools for defensiveness as needed such as noise cancelling headphones or a floppy hat.

## Sleeps Between Mattress and Wall

**Sensory Explanation:** Children with sensory differences tend to have a very difficult time sleeping. The sleep/wake cycle is directly linked to the ability to self-regulate, so those who struggle with self-regulation, often have difficulty sleeping. A child who likes to sleep between the wall and the mattress is likely seeking out deep pressure touch and proprioception to help regulate and sleep.

### Ideas to Help!

- Try using a weighted blanket.
- Try a Lycra™ compression sheet.
- Allow the child to sleep on a pillow cave (like a nest).
- Try a large memory foam type bean bag as an alternative for sleeping.
- Provide full body deep pressure touch prior to bedtime and also weighted ball deep pressure touch.
- Use a vibrating pillow or mattress.
- A memory foam bed topper could be very helpful.
- Have the child sleep in a body sock.

## Sleeps with a Bed Full of Stuffed Animals and Pillows/Blankets

**Sensory Explanation:** Children with sensory differences tend to have a very difficult time sleeping. The sleep/wake cycle is directly linked to the ability to self-regulate, so those who struggle with self-regulation, often have difficulty sleeping. A child who likes to sleep with a bed full of stuffed animals and pillows/blankets is likely seeking out deep pressure touch and proprioception to help regulate and sleep. Also, quite often a child will place the stuffed animals in a very specific order and location…this serves as a sensory anchor to help regulate even more.

**Ideas to Help!**

- Allow your child the time to situate the stuffed animals just like they want to…it can make a big difference in being able to fall asleep.
- Tuck the preferred blankets tightly around the body, as this can add even more deep pressure touch and proprioceptive input.
- Incorporate a weighted blanket or possibly a Lycra™ compression sheet.
- Tight fitting pajamas may also be helpful.
- Try a vibrating pillow or mattress.
- Try using a body sock for sleeping and include a few of the favorite pillows and blankets in the body sock for a cozier feeling.

## Approaches Play or New Textures with Closed Fists or Withdraws Hands

**Sensory Explanation:** Likely sensory defensiveness and over-registration is present with the tactile system. The hands have an enormous amount of tactile receptors, especially the palms; therefore, approaching play or a new tactile experience with a closed fist decreases the amount of tactile input. Also, the first line of defense for the tactile system is to withdraw and not engage in a possibly painful or uncomfortable sensory situation.

**Ideas to Help!**

- Do not force the child to touch something.
- Provide deep pressure touch to the hands and fingers on a regular basis and prior to new texture related activities.
- Place messy/wet textures in a plastic bag for the child to explore first.
- Encourage various types of textures in play, both wet and dry, offering tools such as a shovel or paintbrush. Using a tool first for exploration will help the nervous system become more comfortable with the tactile experience.
- Provide Play-doh® or Moon Sand™.
- Sing songs and encourage deep breathing while engaging in new texture activities.
- Incorporate texture based play through cooking and helping in the kitchen.

### Avoids Eye Contact or Shifts Gaze

**Sensory Explanation:** Eye contact is often misunderstood. When a child is unable to or has a difficult time making eye contact, it is often a sign of overstimulation or dysregulation of the nervous system. The child is actually unable to make the eye contact, as it is too overwhelming to the visual system in everyday situations. Imagine how difficult it may be in a new environment or a stressful situation.

**Ideas to Help!**

- Respect this sensory signal and use it as a gauge as to how regulated the child may be at any given moment. It is likely that you will see an increase in eye contact when the child is in a ready state and regulated.
- Do not insist on eye contact. Lack of eye contact does not equal disobedience. It also does not mean the child is not listening. In fact, the child may be able to listen and process better when NOT having to work so hard on the expected eye contact.
- Let eye contact happen naturally, as it will when the nervous system is regulated.

### Very Destructive

**Sensory Explanation:** A child who is destructive within their environment may be doing this for a few reasons, the most likely reason being a state of sensory dysregulation and a reaction to feeling out of sorts and out of control. The brain/nervous system is simply unable to organize a functional and purposeful response, so instead, just reacts in a sensory seeking fashion. It may also be due to sensory seeking and craving the different aspects of being destructive…such as proprioception, auditory, and visual input that occur during destruction. The other possible explanation is a state of fight or flight.

**Ideas to Help!**

- Maintain a clutter free and organized environment to help with self-regulation and an overall soothing and calming environment.
- Limit the overall amount of sensory input within the environment including decreased auditory and visual input. (Turn off the television, overhead lighting, etc.)
- Encourage regular and frequent doses of input via the power sensations.
- Provide powerful proprioceptive based activities such as toys to bang on, a drum set, or swinging a bat.
- Encourage opportunities to hang from a trapeze or chin-up bar.
- Have the child invert the head on a daily basis.
- Create obstacle courses for powerful doses of sensory input.
- An indoor swing is a great idea.

### Does Not Like Washing Hands

**Sensory Explanation:** There are more sensory components involved with hand washing than one might think. There is the obvious tactile input, but also input from the various types of towels or paper towels used after the washing. There are sounds of the water or echoing bathroom, smells from the soap and the bathroom in general, and the likelihood of a mirror being involved. All of these sensory components create a multi-sensory experience . . . one in which frequent verbal and tactile cueing is taking place.

### Ideas to Help!

- Identify the possible sensory triggers which the child is showing aversion to, such as the feel or smell of the soap. Is the mirror overwhelming?
- Make changes to the activity based on the above findings. For example, if it is the mirror that is overwhelming, wash hands at the kitchen sink instead.
- For home hand washing, let the child decide which type of soap feels and smells the best.
- Sing songs and encourage deep breathing while hand washing.
- If the child is fine with the mirror, encourage funny faces while hand washing.
- Allow the child to wash their hands on their own, and refrain from the hand-over-hand help. This with likely create a negative response from the nervous system.

### Change in Routine Causes Distress

**Sensory Explanation:** A child who struggles with self-regulation relies on structure and predictability to help cope and maintain a ready state throughout the day. When the routine changes, the child's ability to organize and adapt to the new sensory information can be affected.

### Ideas to Help!

- Make every effort to stay on a schedule and routine. This is very beneficial for sensory processing and self-regulation.
- If a change in routine is needed, forewarn the child with plenty of advance notice so he/she can prepare mentally.
- Use a picture book to show the sequence of events for that day.
- Be sure to incorporate additional movement and heavy/hard work breaks during a period of change in routine.
- Provide an oral sensory tool and resistive blowing such as a bubble mountain.
- When a change in routine is anticipated, place extra emphasis on proprioceptive and vestibular activities to help with self-regulation.

### Gags with Textured Foods, Picky Eater, Extreme Food Preferences

**Sensory Explanation:** The mouth is part of the tactile system. This is likely sensory defensiveness/avoidance, and sensory over-registration is occurring with the nervous system. An over-responsive olfactory system is also a very likely factor. Visual processing can also play a role, and the look of the different foods may make the child uncomfortable.

### Ideas to Help!

- Explore various textures to hands and feet on a regular basis to help the tactile system process information.
- Do NOT force the issue with the disliked food item. Let the child explore the food with the hands or a utensil on his/her own terms.
- Respect the need for a very specific temperature of food.
- Encourage the child to chew on gum or an oral sensory tool prior to eating to prepare the mouth for tactile input.
- Encourage the child to jump on a trampoline, bed, hippity hop ball, BOSU® ball, or exercise ball for 5-10 minutes immediately prior to eating.
- Encourage cooking together and playing with food.
- Use a vibrating oral sensory tool or vibrating toothbrush on a regular basis.
- Provide a rescue towel and a rescue bowl at meals. The rescue towel is a wet towel to wipe hands and face as needed and the bowl is to place or spit out food which the nervous system simply cannot handle.

### Dislikes Lotion or Sunscreen Application

**Sensory Explanation:** This is likely due to over-registration and defensiveness of the tactile and/or olfactory senses. The application of the lotion or sunscreen can truly be painful and the smell may cause a systemic response such as nausea.

### Ideas to Help!

- Provide deep pressure touch to the body prior to applying lotion.
- While applying the lotion, use firm pressure, yet not too brisk and quick, which can cause sensory overload.
- Allow the child to help with the application of the lotion as much as possible.
- Stick to natural lotions and products when at all possible, as the scent of chemical-based lotions can be very disruptive to the nervous system.
- Research various natural options for sunscreen, and keep in mind that sunshine is important for D3 absorption.
- Consider the different options, such as spray/mist vs. lotions.
- While applying the lotion, encourage deep breathing. Also, singing songs together can be regulating and a great distraction.
- Consider natural moisturizing baths instead of needing the lotion. Also, place close attention to the soaps and detergents you use, which may be contributing to the dry skin and need for the lotion.

### Hyper-focused on One Type of Toy

**Sensory Explanation:** A child who is very rigid in their toy preference is likely using this as a sensory anchor to help self-regulate. Those with sensory differences tend to thrive on sameness, routine, structure, and predictability. The child can contribute to this feeling by being hyper-focused on a specific toy.

### Ideas to Help!

- Respect this as a sensory signal and do not give the child grief about it.
- If the specific toy has an obvious sensory component, encourage other activities within that same category.
- Regular and frequent doses of the power sensations help with overall self-regulation.
- This specific toy is likely to be the trigger of dysregulation or fight or flight if forced to share. It is best just keep this specific toy as a sensory anchor.

### Nail Trimming Distress

**Sensory Explanation:** The fingertips and fingernail beds are part of the tactile system and have a large number of tactile receptors present. Likely sensory defensiveness and over-registration with tactile system is present. The fact that this task requires being held in place and very close proximity to others can also contribute to the distress.

### Ideas to Help!

- Provide deep pressure touch to hands and feet prior to nail trimming.
- Have the child use Play-doh® with hands prior to trimming.
- Have the child engage in a jumping activity prior to nail trimming of the feet.
- Have the child participate in a heavy/hard work activity immediately prior to the nail trimming.
- Encourage deep breathing.
- Sing songs or play a thinking or guessing game to help distract and avoid fight or flight.
- Try a calm and soothing place for the task such as having the child sit in a squish box or in a sensory retreat.
- Have the child make a tight fist immediately prior to each nail being trimmed. This provides a quick dose of proprioception and deep pressure touch which can be very helpful.

## Hard Time Making Choices and Decisions

**Sensory Explanation:** Making choices and decisions is a lot more complicated than one may think. It requires one to be in a ready state and regulated, which allows for clear thinking and judgment and reasoning to occur. Often those with sensory differences struggle with this because their nervous system is preoccupied with sensation and in a constant state of focusing on self-regulation...not leaving much room in the brain for making decisions and choices.

**Ideas to Help!**

- Respect this as possibly very difficult for your child . . . even a very simple decision.
- Make decisions and choices as simplified as possible. Offering two choices is best.
- It is important to allow for choices and decisions as it is an important part of development, but if you sense that your child is dysregulated or on the brink of sensory overload, refrain from choice and decision making at that moment.
- Encourage decision making and choices when the child is regulated and in the right sensory mood.
- This is an important concept to explain to family members, caregivers, and teachers to help respect the sensory aspect of decision making.

## Hair Cutting Distress

**Sensory Explanation:** This can be explained by sensory defensiveness and over-registration with one or more sensory system. Sensory modulation and/or self-regulation challenges can also be an explanation for the distress. Hair cutting is a multi-sensory activity and also involves social interaction when done outside of the home. There can be various sensory components which can trigger sensory overload or fight or flight. For example, the feeling of the cape around the neck, the sound of the clippers, or the smell of the different chemicals and hair products in the salon can all be sensory triggers.

**Ideas to Help!**

- Take child to the park for 15 minutes prior to the hair appointment. Encourage swinging, climbing, sliding, and hanging upside down from monkey bars, if possible.
- Provide deep pressure touch to head/scalp prior to the hair cutting.
- Encourage deep breathing.
- Allow for use of an oral sensory tool or a fidget toy during the hair appointment.
- Use scissors rather than clippers when possible.
- Cut the child's hair in the comfort of your home, if possible.
- Even one traumatic experience to a hair salon where fight or flight was triggered can create a permanent negative memory for the brain. In this case, you will need to back-track and take baby steps to teach the brain that it is safe.
- Sing songs or play memory or guessing games during the haircut.
- If the child likes the mirror, play a funny faces game as a distraction and to encourage laughing which can help avoid fight or flight.
- Take the time to find a hairdresser that is respectful and patient in regard to the sensory differences.

## Runs Away or Flees Unexpectedly

**Sensory Explanation:** A child who runs away or flees can have more than one sensory explanation. If the child is a sensory seeker and craves sensory input, they may be in a "sensory tunnel" and simply can't resist the running or whatever sensory temptation may lie ahead. Another explanation can be in regard to lack of judgment and safety awareness. The child may truly not process that running or fleeing is dangerous. The third explanation may be that the child is in a state of fight or flight and/or sensory overload.

### Ideas to Help!

- Be very aware of this sensory challenge, and respect it as such. Do not assume it is behavior or attention seeking.
- Assess each situation you are in and determine that it is safe to let the child walk independently; otherwise holding their hand is necessary. Please refrain from using the child leashes.
- Try to determine the sensory reason and act accordingly…such as sensory overload vs. sensory seeking.
- Yelling for the child to stop or calling their name is almost sure to not work. Auditory processing ability in a time like this is disrupted in all three explanations.
- Try having the child sit in a jogging stroller or wagon in busy and chaotic settings.

## Messy Play Is Distressing

**Sensory Explanation:** This can be due to sensory defensiveness and over-registration with the tactile system and possibly olfactory system.

### Ideas to Help!

- Explore various tactile mediums, including dry textures such as sand, kidney beans, lentils, rice, or dry pasta.
- Move from dry textures to wet/messy textures. This is the natural progression for the tactile system.
- Explore the in-between textures such as cooked pasta, Play-doh®, or Moon Sand™.
- Provide deep pressure touch to hands prior to a tactile activity.
- Invite the child to participate in a heavy/hard work activity immediately prior to the tactile activity.
- Never force a child to engage in messy play and resist the temptation to force their little hand in it for even for a second. That one second is enough to cause a systemic reaction (such as nausea) and to trigger fight or flight. The brain will then remember this negative experience and put up a guard to protect the nervous system from future experiences.
- Bubble mountain is a great tool to help prep the nervous system, and the bubbles are an opportunity to experience new texture as well.

### Dislikes Being in a Shopping Cart

**Sensory Explanation:** This can be triggered for a few different reasons, one being the texture and temperature of the cart. The metal or plastic may be very uncomfortable and possibly painful. The vestibular input involved with being in a cart can also be a factor. Another possibility is the fact that the child needs more sensory input and sitting in a shopping cart provides very little input while so much waiting is involved.

### Ideas to Help!

- Bring a blanket and even a small pillow to help protect the child from the texture of the cart.
- Prior to going to the store, take the time to stop at the park or other active movement based play for at least 15-20 minutes; this can be extremely effective in helping the child regulate during the shopping trip.
- When at all possible, shop when the child is with another family member or caregiver. Shopping is just not child friendly.
- If the child is sensitive to movement, rather than having the child ride/move backwards, turn the cart around and push it so the child in the seat is facing forward. The child may handle the motion better this way.
- If the child is old enough and able, let the child ride standing up holding the pushing bar of the cart and you behind them. This also provides a little dose of joint traction to the arms as well as additional proprioception.
- Another option is letting the child push the cart altogether. What a great dose of heavy/hard work!

### Excessively Ticklish or Craves Being Tickled

**Sensory Explanation:** The tickle response is actually a mixed message from the brain of pain and pleasure. The nervous system has a difficult time interpreting the message; therefore, tickling is not recommended at all...especially for a brain that is already having difficulty organizing sensory information. Some children crave being tickled. Typically these children under-register sensory input and crave powerful input in which they can actually feel. This is still not recommended. On the other hand, children who are excessively ticklish are most likely over-registering tactile input.

### Ideas to Help!

- Refrain from tickling (see above).
- Provide frequent full body deep pressure touch.
- Provide frequent proprioceptive activities.
- Use pressure garments, such as Under Armour®, on the upper body and lower body.
- Use Bear Hug™ compression vest.
- Use a weighted blanket as needed.
- Instead of tickling, replace it with gentle rough housing.
- Try replacing tickling with the use of a vibrating toy or pillow.
- Another great alternative is rolling a soft weighted ball over the child's body.

### Gets Upset or Overwhelmed in the Grocery Store

**Sensory Explanation:** The grocery store is absolutely a multi-sensory experience - one also challenged by the fact that it is not kid-friendly by nature and there are SO many rules to follow. There are bright fluorescent light, strange and strong smells, loud sounds, beeps and overhead speakers. The crashing of the carts right when you arrive in the door can be enough to trigger sensory overload and dysregulation for the entire shopping trip.

### Ideas to Help!

- When at all possible, schedule and plan your grocery store trip when your child is at home with the other parent or caregiver, or at school. It really is not worth the sensory distress when you can avoid it.
- If you must bring the child along, be sure you have tools for defensiveness as appropriate for your child's sensory differences.
- If your child struggles with sensory modulation and/or self-regulation, being proactive is the key. For example, have the child wear noise cancelling headphones or earplugs before you even enter the store. Do not wait until the crash of the carts and your child tries to quickly cover their ears and starts crying...avoid this from happening altogether.
- Bring fidget toys and oral sensory tools. Gum or a thick milkshake or smoothie is a great tool to help the child stay regulated in the store.
- Allow for the use of a floppy hat or sunglasses in the store to avoid uncomfortable social interactions and all of the bright lighting.
- Engage your child in the shopping as able, such as lifting and placing the heavy items in the cart or allowing them to hold the list and mark things off as you go. Enlist the child as a helper.

### Hiccups Frequently

**Sensory Explanation:** Hiccups can be caused from crying, laughing, or drinking/eating too fast, but hiccups can also be a neurological sign of sensory overload and dysregulation. Pay close attention to the situation, surroundings, and activities that occur immediately prior to the hiccups.

### Ideas to Help!

- Remove the child from the stimulating environment and provide a sensory retreat if possible.
- Provide full body deep pressure touch.
- Use a weighted blanket.
- Provide a pillow cave or squish box.
- Encourage deep breathing.
- Try bubble mountain or other resistive breathing activities such as a recorder or harmonica.
- Try gentle rhythmical swinging in a hammock or cuddle swing.
- Try inverting the head.
- An oral sensory tool such as a Camelbak® water bottle can be helpful.

### Resists Movement

**Sensory Explanation:** Likely sensory defensiveness/avoidance and over-registration involving the vestibular system and vestibular components including balance and posture. Possible gravitational insecurity and under-registration of proprioception, which decreases body awareness and the ability to determine body in space is another explanation. Resisting movement can also be due to delayed protective reflexes.

**Ideas to Help!**

- Do not force movement. Respect the child's signals to stop.
- Very small doses of movement are beneficial to the brain.
- Begin with vertical (bouncing) type movement, as this is the most tolerated plane of movement for most children.
- Prior to a movement activity, begin with 5-10 minutes of heavy/hard work or other proprioceptive activities such as joint compression or joint traction.
- When working on new linear planes of movement, incorporate full body deep pressure when possible, such as swinging the child in a blanket, or using a cuddle or hammock swing.
- Encourage deep breathing while swinging.
- Incorporate calming and soothing instrumental music while working on tolerated movement.

### Touches Objects Very Lightly

**Sensory Explanation:** This can be explained by possible tactile defensiveness and that the nervous system is on guard and cautious in regard to touching various textures, especially when the object is new and unfamiliar. On the other hand, lack of proprioceptive feedback and body awareness may be the reason. In this case, the child is unable to gauge the amount of pressure used in exploring or touching an object.

**Ideas to Help!**

- Try Theraputty™, clay, or Playdoh® activities.
- If tactile defensiveness is present, begin by having the child explore dry textures, working up to tolerating messy textures. Never force a tactile activity.
- Vibration to the hands using a handheld massager or letting the child use a vibrating pillow can be helpful.
- Provide regular and frequent deep pressure touch to the hands and fingers.
- Provide joint traction and joint compression activities for the arms, such as hanging from a bar or wheelbarrow walking.
- Encourage the child to carry heavy objects and activities requiring grip strength such as opening jars or banging with a hammer or drums.

### Dislikes Bandages

**Sensory Explanation:** Disliking bandages is most likely related to a tactile system that over-registers input. The tactile system is responsible for processing pain and temperature. The feeling of pulling a bandage off is not pleasant for anyone and is that much more difficult for a child who over-registers the feeling of pain. The bandage may also be disliked simply because of the different feeling it creates on the skin - a feeling that the child cannot block out - and the brain is in a constant state of feeling the bandage.

### Ideas to Help!

- If a bandage is not necessary, then skip it and just clean the wound.
- Apply deep pressure touch to the area where the bandage was applied (firm, even pressure); this can help dampen the nerve endings.
- Allow the child to apply the bandage.
- Try non-stick gauze wrapped with self-adhesive wrap instead.
- When removing the bandage, start with a nice warm soaking bath to loosen it.
- Practice wearing bandages when the child is not actually hurt. This will lessen the negative effect of applying the bandage and sensory overload or fight or flight from getting hurt.

### Animal Fear

**Sensory Explanation:** Interaction with animals is multi-sensory, which can cause difficulty with self-regulation. Possible sensory defensiveness/avoidance involving the tactile, auditory, and/or olfactory systems can be the sensory trigger. For instance, dogs bark unexpectedly (auditory) and sometimes jump or lick unexpectedly (tactile) and sometimes have a strong scent (olfactory). Simply the unpredictable factor can be enough to cause the nervous system to be on guard.

### Ideas to Help!

- Do not force the child to pet or interact with the animal, and make sure it is on his/her own terms.
- Read fun and inviting children's books about animals, and visit the local zoo.
- Warn the child when visiting someone with a pet that they may be fearful of, so that he/she has time to mentally prepare.
- When the child is ready to interact with the animal, be sure it involves a very calm animal.
- Try different tools for defensiveness, such as noise cancelling headphones or even tight compression gloves.
- Encourage deep breathing while interacting with an animal.
- Play with an animal and interact yourself; let the child observe. Try not to talk the child through it, just let them observe.

### Stuffs Soft Items in Pajamas to Sleep

**Sensory Explanation:** Children who struggle with self-regulation tend to have difficulty with the sleep/wake cycle. Often additional sensory tools and strategies are needed to support sleep. When a child stuffs pillows, blankets, or stuffed animals into their pajamas, it provides additional proprioception and deep pressure touch, which is calming and regulating and promotes sleep.

### Ideas to Help!

- Let 'em do it, and keep in mind that it is likely helping them sleep.
- Try a Lycra™ compression sheet.
- Try a weighted blanket.
- Tight pajamas that provide some compression can be helpful, as well.
- Provide full body deep pressure touch prior to bedtime.
- A vibrating pillow or mattress can promote sleep.
- Provide an oral sensory tool.
- White noise or soft instrumental music may help.

### Constantly Crashes and Jumps Off of Things

**Sensory Explanation:** Likely difficulty with sensory registration and self-regulation is present. The nervous system is having a difficult time detecting movement and body in space. The intensity involved with jumping and crashing allows for a greater chance for the sensory input to register in the brain…therefore allowing for self-regulation and ability to maintain a ready state.

### Ideas to Help!

- Encourage jumping and crashing! It is a wonderful and healthy activity which provides sensory input, and children LOVE it! Set up a safe area as the crash-and-jump zone.
- Use a BOSU® ball or mini-trampoline indoors with a pillow cave as the safe landing pad.
- Encourage jumping races and hopping like different kinds of animals.
- Use jumping and hopping during transition times getting from point A to point B.
- A hippity hop ball or therapy ball can be helpful.
- An indoor swing, preferably an active type swing (trapeze, bolster swing, platform swing, etc.) would be a great tool.

### Did Not Mouth Objects as a Baby

**Sensory Explanation:** Mouthing toys and objects is an important part of infant development and the ability to self-regulate. It is also how a baby explores and identifies within the environment. A baby that does not or did not do this is likely showing signs of oral sensory and tactile defensiveness. Often, as the nervous system matures, you will see the child mouth toys as they get older and are able to tolerate the sensory experience. It is almost as if the brain and nervous system were making up for lost time, since mouthing objects is such an important part of development.

### Ideas to Help!

- Provide various textured oral sensory tools, as one may be accepted over another.
- Encourage texture based play for the hands and feet. Begin with dry textures and move up to messy textures.
- Encourage other oral sensory based activities such as a bubble mountain or musical instruments such as a harmonica or recorder.
- Provide daily opportunities involving the power sensations, to help promote overall self-regulation.

### Homework: Has Trouble Sitting Still

**Sensory Explanation:** The child may under-register sensory input, especially vestibular and proprioceptive input, both of which are necessary types of sensory input to attend, focus, and promote learning and overall cognition. Most children are asked to sit in a chair to complete homework, but the brain thrives on movement and proprioception to attend and process information.

### Ideas to Help!

- Use a ball chair, hippity hop, or therapy ball instead of a regular chair.
- Allow for at least a 30-minute sensory movement and heavy/hard work break prior to working on homework. Screen time doesn't count!
- Offer a crunchy or chewy snack, such as carrot sticks, pretzels, or string cheese, to be eaten while working on the homework. (Crunchy, chewy snacks promote attention to task.)
- Limit auditory distractions. If unavoidable, then allow for use of headphones, earplugs, or MP3 player with instrumental music while doing homework.
- Provide other oral sensory tools, such as gum or a Camelbak® water bottle for use during homework.
- A vibrating pillow may be helpful.
- A weighted shoulder wrap or lap pad may help.
- If the child must sit in a regular chair, wrap the legs of the chair in Theraband® for resistive pushing and pulling with the lower legs and feet.
- Have the child work on a vertical surface such as an easel.
- Allow the child to stand at the counter to do the homework or lie on the floor on their stomach.

### Hair Brushing Distress

**Sensory Explanation:** The scalp has a large number of tactile receptors. Often a child with tactile defensiveness has difficulty with hair brushing due to the over-reactive sensory receptors on the scalp. A standard hair brush often provides very noxious input to a sensitive and over-reactive scalp.

### Ideas to Help!

- Start with a soft-bristled brush and work your way up to medium or firm-bristled brush.
- Provide deep pressure touch to the head prior to hair brushing.
- If possible, let the child do the brushing, then you can finish up.
- Respect the fact that there can be true pain involved and do not just power through it.
- Sing songs with rhythm and movement during the hair brushing.
- Use essential oils for a de-tangler and for calming olfactory input.
- Encourage deep breathing during the hair brushing.
- Try having the child sit in a squish box for the activity.

### Prefers to "W" Sit

**Sensory Explanation:** W-sitting is when a child sits on the floor with the legs forming a "W" rather than side sitting or "crisscross applesauce". W-sitting is strongly discouraged as it can cause problems for the hip and knee joints. It also doesn't require crossing midline and trunk rotation, which are crucial for brain development. Often when a child W-sits he/she is seeking proprioception to the lower body or has poor trunk or pelvic stability.

### Ideas to Help!

- Encourage side sitting, "crisscross applesauce", lying on tummy, or long leg sitting instead of W-sitting.
- Break this habit as soon as possible! Often a child will W-sit even as an infant. Just manually assist the change of position by moving the legs out in front.
- Have the child sit on a low stool or bench or on a ball chair to encourage posture, pelvic stability and trunk control.
- Have the child engage in frequent vestibular activities which require trunk control such as a BOSU® ball, trampoline, hippity hop ball, or therapy ball.
- Encourage frequent doses of heavy/hard work.
- When cueing the child to switch from W-sitting, keep it fun and playful rather than scolding the child.

## Dressing Difficulty (Including Buttons, Laces, Zippers)

**Sensory Explanation:** Dressing skills require tactile discrimination, body awareness, proprioceptive feedback, and stereognosis of the hands, along with fine motor development and mature prehension patterns. If a child is lacking these sensory skills or developmental skills, learning to dress can be extremely difficult.

### Ideas to Help!

- Practice dressing skills when time is not a factor. If a child is rushed to get dressed, this can create further difficulty for the nervous system in learning the new task. Make it fun, stay positive, and focus on what the child CAN do!
- Practice fasteners with clothing item placed in front of the child first rather than on the body.
- Encourage movement and heavy/hard work play activity prior to getting dressed. This will improve body awareness and proprioceptive feedback for the task.
- Use the forward or backward chaining technique.
- Use Playdoh®, Theraputty™, or clay to work on pinch and grip strength.
- Encourage other fine motor and visual motor activities.
- Refrain from using the hand-over-hand technique.

## Craves Tight and Small Spaces

**Sensory Explanation:** Tight and small spaces often promote body flexion and provide a varied amount of firm pressure to the body and proprioception. All three of these types of sensory input promote self-regulation and can be regulating, calming, and organizing for the nervous system.

### Ideas to Help!

- Respect the need for a safe tight/small space.
- Provide a pillow cave or other form of sensory retreat.
- Provide a squish box.
- Designate and create a safe tight/small space for the child to be used whenever desired.
- Have the child wear compression clothing.
- A weighted blanket or Lycra™ compression sheet can be helpful.
- Provide regular and frequent doses of full body deep pressure touch.
- Try full body massage using a weighted squishy ball.

**Guests or Company in the Home Cause Distress**

**Sensory Explanation:** Social interaction in a group setting is a multi-sensory experience and requires a nervous system which is able to adapt minute to minute. Often auditory, visual, and tactile input is at a very high level and can be difficult for the child to process. The other higher level components include eye contact and communication skills which are also very demanding on the nervous system. Children with sensory differences tend to prefer structure, routine, and predictability…all of which can be disrupted when company is in the home.

**Ideas to Help!**

- Provide earplugs or headphones.
- Have a sensory retreat available for the child if sensory overload occurs.
- Respect the child's possible need to leave the social setting.
- Do not place demands on verbally engaging or making eye contact, as these two skills are extremely difficult for a child who is dysregulated.
- Prior to the guests arriving, help prep your child's nervous system by at least 15-20 minutes of calming vestibular and proprioceptive input.
- Allow the child to play outside in the backyard during the gathering, if possible.

**Dislikes Being Outside**

**Sensory Explanation:** Being outdoors can be difficult for some children, especially those who over-register sensory input and have some type of sensory defensiveness. Being outdoors may be too bright or the unpredictability factor of wind, rain, and loud random sounds (such as a car alarm going off or a siren) can be overwhelming. Tactile defensiveness could also come into play if the child is wearing open-toed shoes or has a difficult time with textures to the hands and feet. Smell can also come in to play while outside; if the child is sensitive to smell they may find the outdoors to be uncomfortable.

**Ideas to Help!**

- Use tools for defensiveness as appropriate for your child. If it is too bright, try sunglasses or a floppy hat. If sound is a factor, use noise cancelling headphones.
- Begin your outdoor experiences in a nice, calm and quiet place.
- Try using a jogging stroller or wagon for your adventures outdoors, and let your child out to explore when they feel comfortable enough to do so.
- Any oral sensory tool could be helpful.
- A fidget toy or other comfort item to bring along when exploring outdoors is a good idea.
- Carry the child if possible, holding the child with firm pressure, and encourage deep breathing together.

## Difficult Time Being Dropped Off at School or Daycare

**Sensory Explanation:** Transitions are often very difficult for children with sensory differences, and being dropped off at school or daycare can be an extra difficult transition since the child is leaving the comfort of home and the comfort of being with the parent or caregiver. To top it off, school or daycare is a place of unpredictable sensory input full or rules and challenges for the nervous system.

### Ideas to Help!

- Do your best not to rush from home to school or daycare; your child can sense the stress and urgency and often it does not leave time to get the important little things done that will help the child self-regulate.
- Bring sensory tools in the car such as a fidget toy, chewing gum or other oral sensory tool.
- Listen to fun and calming music together.
- Use a custom picture board to help visualize the steps involved with the process.
- When you do make the drop off, give a nice firm deep pressure hug with a calm and secure voice. Try not to let your child sense that you are concerned; only show confidence and security in the situation.

## Very Difficult to Calm

**Sensory Explanation:** The ability to self-calm begins in the womb and continues throughout life. If a child has difficulty with self-regulation, he/she will likely need sensory tools and strategies to help calm. The ability to self-regulate relies on an adequate amount of sensory input via vestibular, proprioceptive, and the tactile systems. If the nervous system is having difficulty processing sensory information, difficulty with the ability to self-regulate is very likely affected.

### Ideas to Help!

- Provide an oral sensory tool.
- Provide a weighted blanket or Lycra™ compression sheet.
- Provide a vibrating pillow or other vibrating tool.
- Provide a pillow cave or sensory retreat.
- Use a squish box.
- Use deep pressure touch and bear hugs.
- Do not talk to or make sounds at all when the child is trying to calm down.
- Provide a cuddle swing or hammock swing, swinging in a slow, rhythmic motion.

### Difficulty with Transitions

**Sensory Explanation:** Children tend to thrive and do best with predictability, routine, and structure. Transitions often lack these three traits. Transitions also toss into the mix a change in sensory input and possibly overwhelming amounts of sensory input. Children who struggle with self-regulation, sensory defensiveness, and/or sensory modulation tend to have difficulty with transitioning.

### Ideas to Help!

- Use a visual timer to help the child understand how much time is left before the transition.
- Use a custom picture book or picture board to show the schedule for the day in the order of events. Be sure to break it down into all of its small components.
- Encourage deep breathing and 10-15 minutes of calming vestibular input and proprioception prior to the transition.
- Enlist your child as a helper during the transition, preferably involving heavy/hard work to help self-regulate.
- Try not to rush transitions; this only causes more dysregulation.
- Use sensory tools for defensiveness as appropriate.
- Make sure you have your portable sensory tool bag in the car or on the bus for the child to help regulate.
- Try to make transitions fun, with perhaps fun steps to follow to the car, such as hopping like a kangaroo or bear walking.

### Rigid Clothing Preferences/Dislikes Certain Clothing

**Sensory Explanation:** This is likely due to sensory defensiveness and over-registration of the tactile system. Clothing offers various types of tactile input from the fabric to the tags to the way the clothing lies on the body. Certain clothing will be comfortable, yet other clothing will actually be painful; therefore, the child will not be able to tune out the painful and irritating input on a constant basis.

### Ideas to Help!

- Respect the need to wear only particular clothing.
- Buy seamless and tag less clothing when possible.
- When shopping for clothing, let the child touch it and try it on to determine if his/her tactile system can handle it.
- In the cooler months, wearing compression clothing underneath the clothes can be very helpful and increase the wardrobe choices.
- If a child is fond of a particular type of pants or shirts, I suggest buying a few of them to avoid the day when the item is stained or has holes in it, yet the child is insistent on wearing it.

### Loves to Step or Walk on Things (Toys, Others' Feet, etc.)

**Sensory Explanation:** Walking or stepping on objects provides a powerful dose of proprioceptive feedback to the bottom of the feet, which can feel very good to the nervous system. It can also help a child with body awareness, body in space, motor planning, and balance. This also provides a dose of deep pressure and tactile input, which may be something the child craves. This may serve as a sensory anchor which is calming and soothing to the nervous system.

### Ideas to Help!

- It's okay, let 'em do it! Keep in mind the sensory benefits.
- Of course, be sure the child is not stepping on items that can be harmful, as we know that some children under-register pain and may not feel the sensation as being a little too much.
- Provide regular doses of deep pressure touch to the feet and legs.
- Encourage the use of a vibrating pillow for the feet or a handheld massager for use on the feet.
- Set up fun obstacle courses with various textures for the feet, and have the child do this barefoot.
- Encourage messy play and other texture based play for the feet.
- Set up a path of pillows for the child to walk on.
- Encourage barefoot play on a regular basis.

### Climbs on Others/ Does not Respect Personal Space

**Sensory Explanation:** The child likely under-registers proprioception and lacks body awareness. A child who does not know where their body is in space (due to lack of body awareness) is definitely not going to be able to identify with a "personal bubble" or personal space. Lacking registration of proprioception also creates a need and desire to seek it, such as climbing on others. Climbing on others also provides deep pressure touch which can be very soothing and calming for the nervous system.

### Ideas to Help!

- Increase the amount of heavy/hard work and movement play throughout the day.
- Provide a BOSU® ball.
- Provide a pillow cave.
- Provide compression clothing.
- Use a weighted blanket or lap pad when doing stationary activities.
- Use full body deep pressure touch throughout the day.
- Give lots of bear hugs.
- Try full body massage with a weighted ball or a large therapy ball.
- The steam roller game is a fun idea.
- Offer a squish box on a regular basis.
- Offer a vibrating pillow or handheld massager.

## Constantly Snapping Fingers

**Sensory Explanation:** Snapping fingers provides proprioceptive, tactile, and auditory input to the brain and nervous system. A child may do this to soothe, calm, and regulate. It may also serve as a sensory anchor for the child. Some children snap in a certain rhythm which also provides additional organizing and regulating input.

### Ideas to Help!

- Respect this as a sensory need and let the child do it when it is not disrupting others.
- Encourage the use of a fidget toy.
- Have the child use a handheld vibrating massager.
- Play fun music with which the child can interact and engage in rhythm and movement.
- Try using a metronome and have the child try different beats using clapping, stomping, snapping, etc.
- Provide joint traction, joint compression and deep pressure touch to the hands and fingers on a regular basis.
- Encourage the use of Theraputty™, Playdoh®, or clay.
- Try Theraband® activities for the arms and hands.

## Prefers or Insists on a Ponytail or Hair Pulled Back

**Sensory Explanation:** Having hair pulled back in a headband or ponytail provides tactile and proprioceptive feedback to the head and scalp, so it simply feels good to the nervous system. On the other hand, the child may be challenged with tactile defensiveness where the hair moving around and touching the face is simply unbearable, uncomfortable, or painful.

### Ideas to Help!

- Respect this as a sensory signal and need. Allow for the use of a ponytail or headband at all times if needed.
- Deep pressure touch to the head and face on a regular basis can be helpful.
- The child may be very rigid in the choice of headband or tightness of a ponytail; please respect this and honor the request.

## Lashes Out at Others When They Are Too Close

**Sensory Explanation:** Most likely, tactile defensiveness is present, and unexpected light touch and bumps are interpreted as a threat to the nervous system; therefore, the nervous system reacts in a fight or flight response. This can also occur when a child is in a state of sensory overload, fight or flight, and/or sensory dysregulation. The child is simply in protective mode and any sensory input can be uncomfortable.

### Ideas to Help!

- If standing in a line with a group, be sure the child is at the front or the back of the line, as this decreases the chances of being touched or bumped by 50%.
- In group settings such as circle time, have the child sit on one end or the other, decreasing the chance by 50% that the child will be bumped or touched.
- Have the child wear compression clothing or a Bear Hug™ compression vest.
- Prior to group activities, have the child engage in a heavy/hard work activity to promote self-regulation.
- Allow the child to stand at the back of a line or off to the side of a group at a distance that's safe and comfortable for the child.

## Being Messy at Mealtime Causes Distress

**Sensory Explanation:** This is likely due to sensory defensiveness involving the tactile system; possibly oral sensory defensiveness if the child has rigid food preferences. The child may over-register one or more senses involved with mealtime and the messy component is simply too much to handle.

### Ideas to Help!

- Offer messy play opportunities, but don't force it. Allow for use of tools (such as a paintbrush or play shovel).
- Offer various, new dry textures to experiment with in play.
- Provide deep pressure touch to hands prior to a messy play activity.
- Involve the child in meal prep activities for exposure to textures.
- At mealtime, provide a wet rescue towel to be used as needed to wipe off.
- Do not force eating finger food with hands. Offer a utensil.
- Prior to mealtime, have the child engage in 15 minutes of vestibular and proprioceptive play to prep the nervous system.
- Bubble mountain or other resistive and deep breathing activities right before a meal can help the child regulate.

### Watching Something Moving Causes Dizziness

**Sensory Explanation:** This is most likely related to the vestibular system and/or also the ocular motor system. The vestibular system may be extremely sensitive to movement and is over-responsive. The ocular motor system may also be the cause of this dizziness, in which the motor control of the eyes is not working properly.

**Ideas to Help!**

- Be sure to address the ocular motor issue which your OT or eye professional.
- Be sure to rule out any other medical explanations for this response to movement, as there can be more of a neurological cause.
- With this level of vestibular defensiveness, it is important to involve a sensory integration OT to address the vestibular system.
- At home, begin with vertical vestibular input such as a hippity hop ball, mini trampoline, or gentle bouncing on a therapy ball.
- An indoor swing which incorporates proprioception can be very helpful, such as a hammock swing, cuddle swing, or Lycra™ swing.

### Paces

**Sensory Explanation:** Pacing provides vestibular input in a very rhythmical fashion. Pacing often serves as a sensory anchor and a technique to help self-regulate and to calm and soothe. Pacing sometimes also involves visual input which can be regulating as well.

**Ideas to Help!**

- Let 'em do it, and respect it as a sensory need and a technique to help self-regulate.
- Encourage other rhythmical types of vestibular input such as an indoor hammock swing or cuddle swing.
- A rocking chair may be soothing.
- Encourage deep breathing while pacing, it will help self-regulate more quickly.
- Try singing songs while the child is pacing.
- Offer a squish box or other sensory retreat.
- Try having the child invert their head.
- Encourage the child to hang from a trapeze or pull-up bar.
- Try a BOSU® ball or hippity hop ball.

## Swinging Causes Distress

**Sensory Explanation:** This signal is most likely caused by sensory defensiveness and over-registration involving the vestibular system in one plane of movement or more. The distress may also be related to gravitational insecurity or poor body awareness and the concept of body in space.

### Ideas to Help!

- Respect the signs and signals of an adverse reaction to swinging. Although movement is crucial for brain development, start very slowly...even one minute of slow swinging is beneficial. Stop when the child says to stop.
- Prior to swinging, have the child participate in 15 minutes of heavy/hard work play, such as climbing and hanging.
- Slow rhythmical swinging in a hammock or cuddle swing is a good place to start.
- Encourage deep breathing.
- If the child handles vertical vestibular input well, have the child engage in a jumping or bouncing activity immediately prior to working on swinging.
- Vestibular defensiveness can be very complex; a sensory integration OT consult is recommended in this case.

## Dislikes Wearing Shoes and/or Socks

**Sensory Explanation:** This is very common for many children, sensory challenges or not, but there may be a sensory explanation for it as well. If the child struggles with tactile defensiveness and over-registers tactile input, this could be the reason for disliking shoes and socks.

### Ideas to Help!

- Letting a child go barefoot is actually very beneficial for a number of reasons. It gives proprioceptive feedback to the feet and allows for experiencing new texture.
- When shoes and socks are necessary, take the extra time to make sure the socks are on just right and that the shoes are nice and snug.
- Try seamless socks and let the child choose the texture of sock that feels best.
- Snug-fitting shoes are usually tolerated best since they provide proprioception and deep pressure touch and can dampen the tactile system receptors.
- Provide regular and frequent doses of deep pressure touch to the feet.
- Encourage tactile play involving the feet, such as in sand or a tub of dry beans.
- To eliminate the taking off of shoes and socks in the car, bring the shoes and socks with you and complete this task right before it is time to get out of the car.

### Smells Non-Food Objects and the Surroundings

**Sensory Explanation:** Smelling non-food objects is often used as a sensory anchor and can help a child feel safe and secure in his/her environment and in new surroundings. It is also often the sensory technique used by the child to identify and explore the environment. Often, smells are comforting to a dysregulated nervous system.

**Ideas to Help!**

- Respect this sensory signal, and allow the child do it if needed. Be sure to educate those around the child so they respect it, as well.
- Increase the amount of heavy/hard work type play, as proprioception assists in self-regulation.
- Provide an oral sensory tool and other comforting sensory tools in new settings and situations.
- Allow the child to carry a comforting non-food item as the "go-to" object in social settings and out in the community.
- Try using different essential oils to see if the child gravitates to one vs. another, then place small drops on a comfort item that the child tends to carry around.

### Frequent "Brain Freeze" When Drinking Cold Drinks

**Sensory Explanation:** Children who over-register pain and temperature will detect and feel a "brain freeze" much quicker than the average person. The brain may also be getting the message more quickly and intensely.

**Ideas to Help!**

- Serve drinks at room temperature instead.
- If the child really loves cold drinks, have the child drink it with a super skinny straw (like a coffee straw).
- Apply deep pressure touch and a head compression to help relieve the brain freeze.
- Inverting the head may help.

## Lines Up Objects/Toys

**Sensory Explanation:** This most likely serves as a sensory anchor for the child. Lining up toys or objects is related to the visual system and can be organizing and regulating to a child with sensory processing difficulties. It helps to give a sense of control and organization within a very chaotic brain taking in so much sensory input.

### Ideas to Help!

- Allow the child to line things up!
- Respect the fact that the child needs to do this to feel safe and to have a sense of control and organization within their little world. This can be very soothing and calming for the child.
- Encourage heavy work and movement play. This promotes self-regulation, which in turn can decrease the need to line things up.
- Encourage other types of visual based play such as a marble maze or labyrinth toy.
- Provide other soothing visual tools such as an aquarium or lava lamp to look at.

## Loves to Look at Spinning Objects

**Sensory Explanation:** Looking at spinning objects is most likely a type of sensory anchor for the child. Enjoying looking at spinning objects is related to the visual system and can be organizing and regulating to a child with sensory processing difficulties.

### Ideas to Help!

- Sometimes spinning objects can be quite addictive for a child. Encourage heavy work and movement based activities as an alternative to promote self-regulation.
- Respect the fact that the child needs to do this to feel safe in his/her world and to have a sense of brain organization. This is also likely very calming and soothing for the child.
- Encourage other types of visual based activities which are more engaging, such as building a marble maze or a labyrinth toy.
- Increase the amount of vestibular and proprioceptive input throughout the day to support self-regulation in other ways.

<u>**Smashes and Grinds Face into Stuffed Animals or Soft Objects (Usually Mouth Open)**</u>
**Sensory Explanation:** This provides deep pressure touch and proprioceptive input to the face and mouth. If the child likes to do this with the mouth open, it provides additional oral sensory input. This type of activity is often soothing and calming for the nervous system and may help the child self-regulate.

**Ideas to Help!**

- Let 'em do it, no problem here. Just use this as a sensory signal to provide additional tactile and proprioceptive input and other activities to help self-regulate.
- Full body deep pressure touch could be helpful as well as deep pressure touch to the face.
- Encourage the use of a squish box or pillow cave full of soft pillows and stuffed animals.
- Try a body sock.
- Try a vibrating pillow.
- Try an oral sensory tool.
- Bubble mountain would be a good activity.

<u>**Very Soft-Spoken**</u>
**Sensory Explanation:** This could be happening for a couple of reasons, one being auditory defensiveness and sensitivity. Simply talking louder is uncomfortable for the nervous system. And when one talks quietly it tends to cue the other person to talk more quietly; this is just human nature. The other sensory explanation could be that the child is uncomfortable with social interaction and communication skills.

**Ideas to Help!**

- Respect this as a sensory signal and talk with the child in a quiet setting so that you can have a meaningful conversation not competing with other auditory input.
- Do not force the social interaction and communication; let this happen naturally.
- Encourage movement activities involving listening games or music, as this will help work on auditory processing skills.
- Consider noise cancelling headphones or earplugs as needed for the child if auditory defensiveness is present.

### Hears Every Little Thing

**Sensory Explanation:** This is likely due to auditory defensiveness and over-registration of the auditory system. The auditory system may not be able to filter out the irrelevant sounds; therefore, the child hears every little thing and can be very distracted by it.

**Ideas to Help!**

- Use earplugs or noise cancelling headphones in loud or overwhelming places. (Be sure to keep them with you in a purse or backpack at all times, as you never know when you might need them.)
- In the classroom, have the child's desk placed in the back row and on the left or right side to decrease auditory input.
- Provide an MP3 player with soft instrumental music for use during homework.
- Encourage movement activities on a regular basis. Movement helps the auditory system process. The same cranial nerve processes vestibular and auditory information.

### Fidgets with Something in the Hands Excessively

**Sensory Explanation:** This is common for those who seek out sensory input and/or under-register tactile and proprioceptive input. The child may have difficulty with self-regulation and attention span. Fidgeting with something provides tactile and proprioceptive input, which can help with cognition, behavior, and self-regulation.

**Ideas to Help!**

- Allow for use of a fidget toy/object during school, homework, or times when the child must be sitting still.
- Let the child choose the fidget toy. Each nervous system is different, so something you like might not interest the child.
- Encourage resistive use of hands during play, such as monkey bars, Play-doh®, or bike riding.
- Encourage heavy/hard work and movement play immediately prior to a sit-down activity.
- Try using a ball chair rather than a stationary chair, or allow for the child to do school work lying on the floor or standing and working at a vertical surface (such as an easel).
- Try a balance board for school work and learning activities.

### Leans on Everything

**Sensory Explanation:** Leaning is a way to provide deep pressure to the body and proprioception. Proprioception is regulating and calming to the nervous system. Leaning often indicates a decreased ability to register sensory information, therefore seeking it out. Leaning also may indicate decreased body awareness and the concept of body in space. The child may not be able to feel and register where their body is in space, and leaning on things helps determine this and gives the body proprioceptive feedback.

### Ideas to Help!

- Provide regular doses of deep pressure touch throughout the day.
- Use a weighted blanket or lap pad.
- Have the child wear compression clothing or Bear Hug™ compression vest.
- Encourage wheelbarrow walking for transitions.
- Provide a pillow cave or squish box.
- Encourage joint traction and joint compression activities throughout the day.
- Try using a vibrating pillow or handheld vibrating toy.
- An indoor swing is a good idea.
- Work on prone extension and full body flexion.

### Afraid of the Car Wash

**Sensory Explanation:** An automatic car wash presents itself with multi-sensory and unpredictable input, from the slapping of the windows with the brushes to the powerful and loud spraying of water and the dryer. A child who over-registers sensory input, primarily auditory and/or visual, may have a very difficult time with this experience.

### Ideas to Help!

- Respect this as a true sensory fear and an uncomfortable and quite possibly painful experience.
- Offer tools for defensiveness such as noise cancelling headphones or even a weighted blanket to hide under during the car wash.
- If possible, let the child and a supervising parent or older sibling wait outside of the car wash.
- Encourage deep breathing.
- Give the child plenty of prep time and warning prior to the car wash.

## Does Not Respond to Name When Called

**Sensory Explanation**: This can be explained by auditory processing difficulties and likely under-registration of auditory input. When the child's name is called, the auditory message may be "lost in transit" on the way to the brain. This may be completely unrelated to the ability to hear you. Another explanation may be that the child is focused or preoccupied with another type of sensory input, and simply does not process the information.

### Ideas to Help!

- Be sure hearing loss is ruled out.
- Give the child a second or two to respond to his/her name without saying it a second time…sometimes it takes a little longer to register, and saying it again just disrupts the auditory process.
- Arrange for frequent vestibular/movement activities. Stimulating the vestibular system stimulates the auditory system since they run along the same cranial nerve.
- Do not get angry or frustrated, as the child likely did not really hear you (process the information).
- Decrease the amount of background noise and unnecessary noise within the environment (turn the television off).

## Rubs Head Along Floor (Bull Dozing)

**Sensory Explanation:** A child will often do this in the crawling position. Rubbing the head along the floor while crawling provides proprioceptive input to the head as well as deep pressure touch. There may also be a visual component involved which may be soothing and comforting to the child. A child who does this is most likely using this technique to help self-regulate and organize and calm the senses. This may serve as a sensory anchor for the child.

### Ideas to Help!

- Let the child do it as long as it is not causing harm to the forehead.
- If the child does this a lot, a soft protective helmet could be helpful. The helmet will also provide a dose of proprioception and deep pressure touch in itself, which may be soothing.
- Encourage head compression via head stands or by gentle pressure on the top of the head.
- Have the child invert the head often.
- Encourage frequent heavy/hard work and joint compression and traction activities.
- Try a squish box or pillow cave.
- A snug-fitting hat or compression hat may be helpful.
- Try a weighted hat.

### Staying Seated at School Desk Is Difficult

**Sensory Explanation**: This is likely due to sensory under-registration and possibly sensory modulation difficulty. This is also very common for sensory seekers. Often the nervous system requires some type of movement and proprioception in order to regulate, attend, and maintain a ready state for learning.

### Ideas to Help!

- Use a ball chair or T-stool instead of a chair.
- Allow for frequent movement breaks, especially breaks involving heavy/hard work such as carrying a stack of books or cleaning the chalkboard.
- Use Thera-Band® wrapped around base of chair.
- Provide a fidget toy/object.
- Provide a vibrating pillow to sit on or hold in lap.
- Provide a weighted lap pad.
- Provide an oral sensory tool.
- Allow the child to stand at a vertical working surface such as the chalkboard.
- Try a ball chair with an easel.
- When writing is not required, have the child stand on a balance board for listening and instruction.
- Try a BOSU® ball.
- Allow the child to lie on their stomach on the floor for school work.

### Glazed-Over Look in Eyes

**Sensory Explanation:** The sensory explanation behind this can be a child in a state of sensory overload who simply cannot take in any more input. This can also be a sign of a child on the brink of fight or flight. It may also be related to strictly visual processing, and the glazed-over look is a result of too much visual input.

### Ideas to Help!

- Be sure to rule out any other medical explanation such as seizure activity.
- Use this as your sensory signal to make a change within the environment. Decrease overall sensory input, especially visual.
- Offer a sensory retreat or squish box.
- Encourage deep breathing.
- Apply deep pressure touch or a bear hug.
- Use sensory tools for defensiveness as needed, such as sunglasses or a floppy hat. Noise cancelling headphones may also be helpful to decrease overall input.
- Try calming rhythmical swinging in a hammock, cuddle swing, or Lycra™ swing.

## Jumps in Place All the Time

**Sensory Explanation:** Jumping provides a great amount of proprioceptive input to the lower body as well as vertical vestibular input, both of which can be very regulating and organizing for the brain and nervous system. Sensory seekers tend to do this, as well as children who under-register sensory input overall, since they are able to feel this powerful form of input. This may also serve as a sensory anchor to help self-regulate.

### Ideas to Help!

- It's okay, let 'em do it and know that it is serving a very important sensory purpose.
- Encourage jumping on a trampoline, BOSU® ball, or hippity hop ball.
- Encourage other forms of movement-based play.
- Try other joint compression and joint traction activities.
- Have the child invert their head.
- Set up obstacles courses.
- Try fun games involving animal walking such as crab walking or bear crawling.
- Dance to fun music.

## Very Physical with Others (Difficulty Knowing When to Stop)

**Sensory Explanation**: This may be due to sensory under-registration, particularly involving the proprioceptive system. The child may be unable to gauge the amount of pressure and force used in play and interaction. It is also very possible that the child has decreased body awareness and a hard time identifying body in space.

### Ideas to Help!

- Encourage heavy/hard work activities throughout the day.
- Allow for jump-and-crash activities.
- Use full body deep pressure touch often throughout the day.
- Provide compression clothing for upper and lower body.
- Use wheelbarrow walking as a transition.
- Provide a pillow cave.
- Encourage resistive activities for the hands such as Play-doh® or Moon Sand™.
- Try a squish box.
- Encourage joint compression and joint traction activities.
- Try a resistance tunnel.
- A body sock is a good idea.

### Pulls Out Eyelashes

**Sensory Explanation:** This can be explained as a tactile seeking activity or sensory anchor, although it is considered a self-injurious behavior. A child who does this likely under-registers pain. It is actually soothing to the child and helps self-regulate.

**Ideas to Help!**

- Establish when the child does this most and adapt/modify the situation if possible. If this is done when the child is sitting still or watching TV, decrease the amount of sedentary time.
- Encourage the use of a fidget toy, and try to find one that has a pinch-and-pull factor.
- Provide regular opportunities for use of clay, Theraputty™, or Playdoh®.
- Try an oral sensory tool.
- Encourage the use of a squish box.
- Offer frequent doses of vestibular and proprioceptive play throughout the day.
- Try a handheld vibrating toy or a vibrating pillow.

### Does Not Feel Pain Like Others

**Sensory Explanation**: Pain is interpreted by the nervous system via the tactile system. If sensory under-registration is present, a child may not register or feel pain like others. Some children may not feel pain at all.

**Ideas to Help!**

- Be very aware of this in regard to safety. If you observe a traumatic fall or injury, it may be best to have it looked at by a doctor even if the child does not respond to the painful stimuli.
- Be sure the hot water faucet temperature is not set too high, as the child may not register the feeling of hot and may burn him/herself.
- Educate family, caregivers, and teachers in regard to this sensory difference.
- Encourage frequent daily doses of input via the power sensations to help overall sensory processing.
- Encourage tactile based play in various textures.
- Encourage full body messy play.

### Sleeps with Pillow Over Face

**Sensory Explanation:** A child who does this may be blocking out visual and auditory input, as even the slightest bit of noise or light can disrupt the nervous system for sleeping. The child may also be doing it to provide deep pressure touch and proprioception to the face and head.

### Ideas to Help!

- Try earplugs or an eye mask for sleeping.
- Thoroughly assess the bedroom environment to determine any changes that can be made in regard to further decreasing sound or light in the room.
- Try white noise or soft instrumental music.
- Provide deep pressure touch to the head and face at bedtime.
- Try a weighted blanket or Lycra™ compression sheet for additional help with self-regulation for sleeping.

### Bounces on Bottom Across the Floor

**Sensory Explanation:** Bouncing like this provides a great amount of proprioceptive input to the lower body and spine as well as providing vertical vestibular input, both of which can be very regulating and organizing for the brain and nervous system. Sensory seekers tend to do this, as well as children who under-register sensory input overall, since they are able to feel this powerful form of input. This may also serve as a sensory anchor to help self-regulate.

### Ideas to Help!

- Let 'em do it, and know that it is great for the brain and nervous system.
- Encourage other types of vertical vestibular input such as a hippity hop ball, Rody, or a trampoline.
- Try a BOSU® ball.
- Therapy ball activities may be helpful.
- Encourage other forms of joint traction and compression.
- Provide full body deep pressure touch often.
- Try a body sock.
- Try a squish box.
- An indoor swing with a proprioceptive component would be a great tool, such as a cuddle swing or hammock swing.

### Extreme Preference with Temperature of Food/Drink

**Sensory Explanation**: Temperature is regulated through the tactile system, and if a child demonstrates tactile defensiveness, he/she may be sensitive to temperature as well. The tactile and temperature receptors located inside the mouth may be over-responsive. The child may have an aversion to only cold or hot or to both.

### Ideas to Help!

- Respect the need for foods or drinks at a particular temperature. The child is not just being demanding.
- Have the child engage in various tactile activities for the hands, feet, and full body. This will facilitate processing of the tactile system overall.
- Using a straw for cold drinks can be very helpful.
- Serving food or drink at room temperature is often accepted better by the nervous system.

### Grinds Teeth

**Sensory Explanation:** Teeth grinding provides proprioception to the jaw joints. This often serves as a sensory anchor which is calming and regulating for the nervous system. Some children may even like the sound created by doing this. (Not me! It makes me cringe writing this!)

### Ideas to Help!

- Nighttime teeth grinding is the most common; a mouth guard is a good idea to protect the teeth.
- During the day, encourage other types of oral sensory tools.
- A Camelbak® water bottle would be a great tool.
- Try a bubble mountain.
- Encourage chewy and crunchy snacks.
- Try a vibrating oral sensory tool.
- Provide deep pressure touch to the cheeks.

### Overheats Very Easily

**Sensory Explanation:** Temperature is regulated through the tactile system, and if there is difficulty with tactile processing, the temperature gauge and regulator of the body may not be working well either.

### Ideas to Help!

- When outdoors, have the child wear a floppy hat or fisherman's hat.
- Be sure that the child is dressed for the weather with the special temperature needs being addressed.
- Be sure that the child is wearing breathable clothing in the summer.
- Always have water available for the child to drink.
- Pay attention to the child's time outdoors and in the sun; often, he/she will overdo it if not monitored.
- Encourage tactile based play, especially full body messy play to help overall tactile processing.

### Sucks Stomach in as Far as Possible, Then Puffs it Out

**Sensory Explanation:** Doing this provides proprioceptive input to the core/trunk of the body. This may be very regulating and soothing to a child.

### Ideas to Help!

- It's okay, let 'em do it and respect it as a sensory need.
- Encourage other proprioceptive based activities.
- Try full body deep pressure touch.
- Try full body massage using a weighted soft medicine ball.
- Roll a large therapy ball firmly over the child's body while they are lying on the floor.
- Try a squish box or pillow cave.
- Try a resistance tunnel.
- Try a body sock.

## Fireworks, Parades, Movie Theaters, Gymnasiums Cause Distress

**Sensory Explanation:** The above mentioned environments are multi-sensory, but the greatest amount of overwhelming stimuli is auditory input in frequencies of sound that are not typically heard on a daily basis. The sounds are often unexpected bursts of noise, which can be difficult to process. Sensory defensiveness and an over-responsive auditory system are likely involved.

### Ideas to Help!

- Always have earplugs or noise cancelling headphones available when out in the community.
- Be proactive and have the child use the earplugs or headphones prior to being over-stimulated and dysregulated.
- Stop at the park for 10-15 minutes of vestibular and proprioceptive input to help prepare the auditory system.
- Avoid these types of activities until your child's nervous system has matured more and can tolerate these multi-sensory experiences.
- Many towns offer sensory-friendly movie experiences. See if your town does this.
- Bring along a portable sensory retreat such as a jogging stroller with a blanket to cover it up for a safe place for your child to retreat to.
- Use other tools for defensiveness as needed such as sunglasses or a floppy hat.
- Encourage the use of an oral sensory tool such as a Camelbak® water bottle or Camelbak® backpack.
- Bring along a fidget toy or other comfort item.

## Being in a Restaurant Causes Distress

**Sensory Explanation:** Restaurants are a multi-sensory experience AND often require the child to sit still for long periods of time (which does not help the situation). Auditory, olfactory, and visual stimuli are the primary sources of overwhelming input. Restaurants can be difficult for a sensory seeker or an avoider, as well as those children with oral aversion and feeding challenges.

### Ideas to Help!

- A quick stop at a playground before going out to eat can be a tremendous help to the nervous system…10-15 minutes of movement and heavy/hard work type play.
- If the weather isn't conducive, indoor play at home before the outing will work, such as an indoor swing, BOSU® ball, hippity hop ball, or wheelbarrow walking.
- Earplugs, noise cancelling headphones, and a floppy fisherman's hat and sunglasses are good tools to have with you.
- Let the child go under the booth as a cozy little sensory retreat.
- If the choice is available, choose a corner table or booth.
- Be sure to bring along a fidget toy or other sensory tools to occupy the child's time.
- Dine during slow business hours, such as an early dinner.
- Choose family-friendly restaurants and avoid a restaurant where additional waiting is required in the lobby area.
- This is a great time to allow the child to have a smoothie or milkshake, for the resistive sucking through the straw. This can help self-regulation tremendously.

## Loves to Be Wrapped Tightly in Blankets

**Sensory Explanation:** Being wrapped tightly in a blanket provides calming, organizing, and regulating deep pressure touch and proprioceptive input. This is a very therapeutic type of sensory input, especially those who struggle with self-regulation. This can also be very helpful for a child in a state of fight or flight or sensory overload.

### Ideas to Help!

- The more often you wrap them the better! This is excellent for the nervous system.
- Provide a pillow cave.
- Provide a weighted blanket or lap pad.
- Provide full body deep pressure touch on a regular basis.
- Give frequent bear hugs.
- Have the child wear upper and lower body compression clothing, possibly a Bear Hug™ compression vest.
- Provide a squish box.
- Provide full body massage using a weighted soft medicine ball.
- When the child is wrapped in the blanket, provide additional input by firmly rolling a therapy ball over the body.
- Try a body sock or resistance tunnel.

## Hair Pulling on Self

**Sensory Explanation**: Although this seems painful, it likely is not painful to a child who under-registers tactile input and pain. It often indicates sensory under-registration and difficulty with self-regulation. It is considered a maladaptive, self-stimulatory behavior, but it is regulating and calming to the child.

### Ideas to Help!

- Allow for frequent movement and heavy/hard work activities throughout the day.
- Have the child wear compression clothing or a Bear Hug™ compression vest.
- Provide a fidget toy/object for hands. Let the child choose the toy. Vibrating toys are very effective.
- Provide Play-doh® or Moon Sand™.
- Provide full body deep pressure touch throughout the day.
- Try a compression type hat or beanie.
- Try oral sensory tools or a bubble mountain.
- Try joint compression and joint traction activities.
- Encourage full body messy play and other texture based play to improve tactile processing.

### Scratches Self/ Picks at Skin

**Sensory Explanation**: This often indicates sensory under-registration and difficulty with self-regulation. It is considered a maladaptive, self-stimulatory behavior, but it is regulating and calming to the child. Often the child will pick or scratch self to the point of creating a sore or injury.

### Ideas to Help!

- Provide a fidget toy/object for hands.
- Encourage heavy/hard work play, especially resistive play with the hands such as Play-doh®, clay, or Moon Sand™.
- Have the child wear compression clothing on areas where he/she tends to scratch or pick.
- Encourage tactile play with hands, feet, and whole body using various textures such as sand, rice, kidney beans, finger paints, pudding, and play-foam soap for the bathtub.
- Incorporate frequent doses of input from the power sensations throughout the day to help with self-regulation.
- Try vertical vestibular input activities such as a trampoline, BOSU® ball, or hippity hop ball.
- Try a vibrating handheld massager or vibrating pillow.

### Clothing, Shoes, and/or Belt Must Be Worn Very Tightly

**Sensory Explanation:** Wearing clothing and shoes tightly provides proprioception to the body throughout the day. It is a signal that the child is craving calming and regulating input and needs additional proprioception. This often occurs with sensory under-registration, decreased body awareness, and self-regulation difficulties.

### Ideas to Help!

- Acknowledge the fact that the child is wearing his/her clothing and shoes like this for a reason. If it is not cutting off circulation and leaving pressure areas that last more than 20 minutes when the article of clothing is removed, then let him/her do it!
- Have the child wear upper and lower body compression clothing, possibly a Bear Hug™ compression vest.
- Provide a Camelbak® water backpack to be worn during the day.
- Provide a weighted belt.
- Provide full body deep pressure touch in frequent doses.
- Try a body sock or resistance tunnel activities.
- Frequent doses of joint traction and compression would be helpful.

### Dislikes Straps and Seatbelts

**Sensory Explanation:** This is most likely related to tactile defensiveness and tactile over-registration. It can also be related to overall self-regulation and sensory modulation difficulties. Being in the car or car seat involves so many sensory components that the seatbelt or strap in the car seat is just enough to cause sensory distress.

### Ideas to Help!

- Try the Seatbelt Comfort Device®, which improves the positioning of the seatbelt.
- Try padded seatbelt strap covers.
- Try a Blankid Buddy®.
- Use a travel pillow.
- Bring along other sensory tools such as an oral sensory tool or fidget toy.
- Try a weighted lap pad or vibrating pillow.

### Walks on Toes (Toe Walking)

**Sensory Explanation:** Toe walking is often a sensory signal that the child is trying to self-regulate. This often serves as a sensory anchor. Toe walking increases proprioceptive feedback and in turn promotes self-regulation. This can become a habit for the child due to muscle memory and how the brain learns specific gait patterns.

### Ideas to Help!

- Be sure this is assessed by a PT or OT to determine any other possible factors contributing to the toe walking such as muscle tone or decreased range of motion.
- Use weighted shoe pockets or weighted belt.
- Encourage jumping activities such as trampoline, BOSU® ball, hippity hop ball, marching, hopping, and skipping.
- Encourage walking up hills.
- Encourage climbing slides.
- Try other types of joint traction and compression activities.

### Excessive Questioning About Future Events/Places/Times/People

**Sensory Explanation:** Children with sensory differences thrive on routine, structure, and predictability. The excessive questioning is likely a way to help the child feel secure and safe in preparation for the upcoming event or visit with a new person. It will help to create a visual picture in their head of what to expect.

### Ideas to Help!

- Be very patient and answer the questions. What may seem unnecessary to you is especially important for the child.
- Create a custom picture book or visual schedule to help with the series of events or upcoming schedule.
- Show pictures to the child of the new person or place if possible.
- If perhaps the upcoming event is a place you can preview, such as a new gymnastics class, do this a couple of days beforehand to help prep the child's nervous system.

### Bangs Toys and Objects Excessively and Intensely

**Sensory Explanation:** Banging of toys and objects provides proprioception to the arms and upper body, and this can promote self-regulation. It also provides additional proprioceptive feedback to the joints of the arms, which is needed for body awareness and if the child under-registers sensory information. In other words, it feels good to the body because the child can feel it, unlike if it were done more gently.

### Ideas to Help!

- Put some earplugs in and let 'em bang! It really is good for the nervous system.
- Use full body deep pressure touch throughout the day.
- Encourage resistive play for the arms, such as push-and-pull activities.
- Encourage wheelbarrow walking.
- Encourage hanging from bars.
- Have the child wear compression clothing.
- Provide a pillow cave.
- Try a drum set.
- Try a body sock or resistance tunnel.

## Falls Intentionally Frequently

**Sensory Explanation:** Falling provides full body proprioception and when a child has difficulty self-regulating, he/she often requires and seeks out proprioceptive input. This may be observed even more frequently in stressful or new situations or during a transition from one thing to another.

### Ideas to Help!

- Provide full body deep pressure touch when the child is demonstrating this sensory signal.
- Provide gentle joint traction to the arms.
- Have the child wear compression clothing, possibly a Bear Hug™ compression vest.
- Encourage the child to replace the falling with hopping, marching, and skipping.
- Encourage wheelbarrow walking.
- Encourage the child to hang from a stationary bar.
- Provide tools for defensiveness as needed if it seems there are other types of sensory input causing the sensory dysregulation (such as noise cancelling headphones).
- Try an oral sensory tool to help the child self-regulate.

## Dentist Causes Extreme Fear and Distress

**Sensory Explanation:** Visiting the dentist is a multi-sensory experience which also involves unexpected sensory input and often new and painful experiences. Strange sounds, strange smells, and an enormous amount of oral sensory input and tactile input are involved.

### Ideas to Help!

- Begin by a trip to the park or allow at least 15-20 minutes of movement and heavy/hard work play immediately before going to the dentist appointment.
- Have the dentist place the weighted x-ray blanket on the child as soon as they get in the chair and leave it there the entire visit for proprioception to help calm.
- Offer earplugs or noise cancelling headphones, if needed.
- Provide a calming fidget toy/object during the visit.
- Provide an MP3 player with calming or favorite music.
- Access the printable handout on this topic from *ASensoryLife.com* and also give a copy to the dentist staff.

### Tooth-brushing Causes Distress

**Sensory Explanation**: Tooth-brushing involves oral sensory and tactile input, which can be overwhelming to the nervous system if tactile or oral sensory defensiveness is present. The adverse response can be from the feeling of the toothbrush and/or the taste and smell of the toothpaste.

### Ideas to Help!

- Use a baby toothbrush with very soft bristles and no toothpaste first, even if it is an older child. Then work your way up to using toothpaste.
- Try various flavors of toothpaste.
- Let the child be involved from the first step of the task and let him/her also brush own teeth (you can finish).
- Provide a resistive blowing activity such as a bubble mountain right before tooth-brushing.
- Have the child chew gum or eat a chewy or crunchy snack right before tooth brushing to prep the mouth.
- Try a vibrating tooth brush or spin brush.
- Sing songs to your child and let the child dance a little during the task.

### Makes Loud, Repetitive Sounds When Someone is Talking or in a Chaotic Environment

**Sensory Explanation:** This is most likely done to tune out the sensory input around the child. It can be a technique to help self-regulate and avoid sensory overload. It may also be a way to express the fact that the social interaction or setting is overwhelming and uncomfortable. Loud vocal sounds, especially repetitive sounds, can serve as a sensory anchor to calm and soothe the child.

### Ideas to Help!

- Use this as your sensory signal to change the environment and decrease the amount of sensory input to avoid sensory overload or fight or flight.
- Encourage the use of noise cancelling headphones.
- Try an MP3 player with soothing music.
- Do not insist on eye contact or social interaction if the child is showing signs of dysregulation and sensory overload.

## Seeks Vibration to Mouth

**Sensory Explanation**: Vibration to the mouth activates tactile receptors as well as provides proprioceptive input to the jaw. This type of input can be very helpful in self-regulation and providing additional oral sensory input which is often calming and organizing for the brain.

**Ideas to Help!**

- Allow for use of an electric toothbrush throughout the day.
- Provide resistive blowing activities such as a bubble mountain.
- Provide chewy and crunchy foods.
- Provide chewing gum.
- Encourage sucking thick liquids or yogurt/pudding through a straw.
- Provide an oral sensory tool, possibly one that vibrates.

## Rubs Body on Surfaces Excessively

**Sensory Explanation**: Rubbing the body along things provides sensory feedback to the body and helps to regulate the brain. It provides proprioceptive feedback and deep pressure touch, which in turn can be organizing and regulating for the brain. It also helps with the feeling of body in space and body awareness.

**Ideas to Help!**

- Provide frequent doses of full body deep pressure touch.
- Have the child wear compression clothing, possibly a Bear Hug™ compression vest.
- Encourage heavy/hard work activities throughout the day.
- Provide a weighted blanket or lap pad.
- Provide a squish box.
- Provide a pillow cave.
- Try a body sock or resistance tunnel.
- Try wrapping the child tightly in blanket and then rolling a therapy ball over the body.
- Encourage full body messy play.
- Play the steam roller game.
- Encourage dancing and yoga moves.

### Writing Causes Great Distress

**Sensory Explanation:** Handwriting requires a number of sensory and developmental skills to be in place. Fine motor and visual motor skills are involved as well as visual perception. Shoulder girdle stability and prehension patterns of the hand must also be functional. Proprioceptive awareness of the hands and arms plays a very large role in being able to write functionally.

### Ideas to Help!

- It is a good idea to have this assessed by an OT to determine the areas possibly causing the distress and delay.
- Encourage use of clay, Theraputty™, and Playdoh®.
- Allow for very short periods of handwriting with frequent breaks.
- Try a built up handle for the pencil or a butterfly pencil grip.
- Offer an oral sensory tool during handwriting activities.
- Try a ball chair or T-stool for handwriting tasks.
- Try an easel or other vertical writing surface.

### Drools Excessively

**Sensory Explanation:** Excessive drooling can be due to lack of muscle tone and/or proprioceptive awareness of the mouth/jaw structures and muscles.

### Ideas to Help!

- Provide an oral sensory tool.
- Allow for use of an electric toothbrush throughout the day.
- Encourage resistive blowing activities such as a bubble mountain.
- Provide chewy and crunchy foods.
- Provide chewing gum if the child is able.
- Encourage sucking thick liquids or yogurt/pudding through a straw.
- Offer smoothies frequently and milkshakes occasionally.

### Prefers Foods with Intense Flavor

**Sensory Explanation**: Possible sensory under-registration of taste and smell. Foods with intense flavor can also be regulating for the nervous system and are often craved by children with sensory processing difficulties.

### Ideas to Help!

- Of course, there is really nothing wrong with someone liking intense flavor. Just respect it as a sensory need and know that it indeed may be helping them self-regulate.
- Offer various olfactory (smell) stimuli in the form or essential oils or soak cotton balls with lemon, vanilla extract, peppermint, etc. Often, children who seek intense flavor also benefit from aroma type therapy.
- Try other oral sensory tools such as a bubble mountain.

### Fearful, Anxious, or Aggressive with Light or Unexpected Touch

**Sensory Explanation**: This is likely related to sensory defensiveness and an over-responsive tactile system, which creates a fight or flight response. The nervous system and brain perceive the tactile input as dangerous and painful, therefore responding in a defensive fashion.

### Ideas to Help!

- Only touch the child with firm pressure touch. Avoid light touch kisses and light touch input, such as softly rubbing the child's arm or lightly touching the hair.
- Provide frequent doses of deep pressure touch and bear hugs.
- Have the child wear compression clothing.
- Encourage tactile play with various mediums of wet and dry textures to hands and feet, working first with dry textures and moving up to messy.
- Be sure that the child's teacher and caregivers are aware of the sensory difference.

### Dislikes Wearing a Jacket

**Sensory Explanation:** This can be explained by either tactile defensiveness or possibly auditory defensiveness. A jacket feels very different on the body and may be uncomfortable or painful to the neck area or wrists. It may also be too loud in regard to the sound of the fabric when the child moves.

### Ideas to Help!

- When buying or choosing a jacket, be sure to involve the child and let them decide which coat feels okay.
- Try to determine if the discomfort is from the feel of the coat or the sound of the coat.
- Eliminate the noise factor by getting a fleece type coat.
- Compression type clothing underneath the coat may be helpful.

### Literally Bounces off Walls (Pushes off One, Runs to Other Side, Repeats)

**Sensory Explanation:** A child who likes to do this is most likely using it as a way to self-regulate and organize the brain. This can feel great to the nervous system, especially for a sensory seeker or a child who under-registers sensory input overall. It can also feel good to a child who struggles with sensory modulation. Doing this provides vestibular and proprioceptive input.

### Ideas to Help!

- Encourage other types of powerful movement based play such as an indoor swing.
- A trapeze swing would provide additional proprioception.
- Try a BOSU® ball or hippity hop ball.
- Use a trampoline or mini-trampoline.
- Use a pillow cave or large bean bag as a safe crash pad for big jumps.
- Try a resistance tunnel or body sock.
- Provide a squish box.
- Limit screen time to no more than two hours total per day.

### Squeezes Others' Cheeks

**Sensory Explanation:** A child who does this is likely craving proprioceptive input and tactile feedback to their own hands. It may also be an affectionate way for the child to interact, not realizing that it may be uncomfortable to the other person.

### Ideas to Help!

- Provide a fidget toy chosen by the child.
- Offer Theraputty™, Playdoh®, or clay.
- Encourage hanging from a bar and other push-and-pull activities for the hands.
- Try a handheld massager.
- Encourage Theraband® activities.

Now that you have read through all of the sensory signals, you probably learned quite a bit about yourself, your child or children, along with all sorts of other people who popped into your head! It is completely normal and nothing to be concerned about if you could personally identify or apply numerous sensory signals to your child or yourself. **We all have sensory preferences and we all have sensory differences,** and this is to be expected. At times, however, there are so many sensory differences that it impacts one or more areas of development and the quality of life.

Are you ready to learn just a little bit more?

Don't worry...I have simplified it just like the rest of the handbook!

# Sensory in a Nutshell!

**A little bit more than just the sensory signals, not too much to overwhelm you, just enough to see the big sensory picture. Here are the 15 topics I will discuss in nutshell fashion.**

1. There are a few sensory words that will help you to grasp the concept of sensory integration and sensory processing.
2. A sensory meltdown is different than a standard meltdown, and how you handle it is also different.
3. Children naturally want to please others and do not intend to misbehave. All they really want is to be accepted and loved. Before reacting with a reprimand or a punishment, or making an assumption of "behavior", consider a sensory tool or strategy.
4. Sensory anchor is a more respectful and positive concept than the term "stimming"... which has a negative feel to it.
5. Fight or flight and triggering the sympathetic nervous system happen more often for children with sensory differences, and sometimes for no obvious sensory reason.
6. A child with sensory differences may spend the entire day just trying to achieve and maintain ready state and is consumed with trying to self-regulate. This can be exhausting for the child.
7. Sensory input is powerful, and understanding a child's sensory needs and differences can truly change the quality of life for that child.
8. The brain responds best to purposeful and meaningful activities. A rigid sensory diet/home program is not nearly as likely to be carried over long term as naturally incorporating sensory activities into the day. Sensory needs and challenges can change on a day to day basis. One technique, tool, or strategy may work one day and not the next.
9. Vestibular, proprioceptive, and tactile input are the three most important sensory systems to support. They are the foundation to all development.
10. To truly support your child's development, sensory systems and overall nervous system development, it is critical to see the big picture of health and how to support it best.
11. Proprioception is your friend and go-to sensory system.
12. The vestibular and auditory systems have an incredible connection. Use this to your advantage.
13. The massive addiction and overuse of screen time by children is depriving the nervous system of critical sensory input for proper development.
14. Sensory modulation is how our brains sort out and organize all of the sensory input. This is a very common area in need of support for children with sensory differences.
15. The vestibular system is the most complicated, yet most important sensory system to understand. The brain thrives on movement to attend and process information. Keep this in mind when it comes to learning and academics.

# Topic #1
## Sensory 101…The big words, simplified.

**Sensory Processing:** This is how the brain takes in all sensory input. There are 7 sensory systems with 7 different pathways to the brain. It really is just that…processing of sensory input. It is not to be lumped into something that is a problem or disorder. Sensory processing is a basic and foundational function of the nervous system.

**Sensory Integration:** This is the more complex end product of sensory processing. It is the point of nervous system development when the brain integrates all of the senses with a functional outcome. This is the big picture. It is the integration of all of the senses and the brain putting it all together.

**Proprioception:** Any push (joint compression) or pull (joint traction) on a joint, or muscle group that is activated provides proprioceptive input. This can be achieved through almost any movement of the body, and even greater when it involves "heavy/hard work". Body awareness, body in space, and motor planning rely on proprioceptive input for proper development.

**Interoceptors:** These sensory receptors are located inside the body, primarily the gut. It is how we detect that we are full or hungry, or when we need to go to the bathroom.

**Tactile:** The tactile system includes all of your skin as well as inside the mouth, nose, and ears. Tactile input can be in the form of light touch or firm touch. The tactile system is also responsible for detecting and processing pain and temperature.

**Deep pressure touch:** Deep pressure touch is a form of tactile input, yet stands alone in regards to sensory integration. It is the most tolerated form of tactile input and tends to be the most regulating, calming, organizing, and soothing for the nervous system. It is very unlikely for one to be defensive to deep pressure touch.

**Vestibular:** Think movement and balance when you hear this word. It is the most complex and powerful sensory system and involves many different planes (directions) of movement. The word comes from the fact that there are 3 vestibules within the inner ear which detect all of the different planes of movement and determine body in space.

**Self-regulation:** The ability to self-regulate is constant and is how we maintain a functional state of alertness throughout the day. It is also responsible for transition to sleep and awake. Self-regulation impacts mood, behavior, attention, and emotions. Self-regulation requires an adequate amount of various types of sensory input throughout the day to regulate. Dysregulation is the state of the nervous system when it is disorganized and out of sorts.

**Over-registration:** This can occur with one or more sensory systems. It is when the brain detects too much sensory information and is unable to ignore or sort out the irrelevant input. This is when too many sensory receptors are firing at once with one or more of the sensory systems. Those who over-register tend to avoid sensory input, especially multi-sensory input.

**Under-registration:** This can also occur with one or more sensory systems. It is when the brain does not detect enough sensory information and the brain craves more and more, not getting enough sensory nutrition. Those who under-register almost constantly crave very intense sensory input.

**Sensory Modulation:** Please refer to Topic #14 below, as this topic is a bit more complex.

## Topic #2

### A Sensory Meltdown vs A Standard Meltdown

The word **"meltdown"** is one of the most frequently used terms for children with sensory differences. It is also likely the greatest challenge a parent faces with any child....and a whole new ballgame when a child struggles with sensory processing and self-regulation.  A **standard meltdown** may be referring to a child who is kicking and screaming and biting or spitting...or a child who simply can't stop crying....or a child reacting to a situation in a disruptive and aggressive manner...a child seeking attention...a child acting out to get their way....or simply losing all emotional control.

**On the other hand...when you throw sensory processing challenges and difficulty with self-regulation into the mix...you have a completely different scenario.**


**Children inherently want to please.  They do not want to misbehave or get into trouble.**
This concept is very important to remember when talking about sensory meltdowns. The sensory meltdown is often mistaken for attention seeking or spoiled behavior or simply the child trying to get what he/she wants out of the situation.  This may be true in a few cases, but it is often much more deeply rooted than that.  Here are some of the most common reasons a child may have a sensory meltdown....

- Sensory overload

- Dysregulation and the inability to maintain self-regulation and a ready state

- A fight or flight response to sensory overload, yet mistaken for a standard, behavior driven meltdown

- The inability to cope with a new or challenging situation

- Inability to communicate wants and needs

- Difficulty with transitions

- Lack of sleep or overly tired

- Lack of proper nutrition or too much of the wrong food

- Change in routine


Visit this page on my website for ideas on how to help a child during a sensory meltdown:

http://asensorylife.com/sensory-meltdowns.html


**Other related pages for more information:**

http://asensorylife.com/sensory-overload.html

http://asensorylife.com/self-regulation.html

http://asensorylife.com/fight-or-flight.html

## Topic #3

## Children want to please. Don't assume behavior, think sensory first.

After reading through the sensory signals in this book, I hope you have discovered that many of the things you might have considered behavioral, are actually sensory driven. Yes, all kids can be stinkers, and that is perfectly normal and wonderful! It is part of the development of the "sense of self". I know it can be incredibly difficult to determine if the trigger is sensory or behavior sometimes. Here is an acronym I created to help you...

## S.E.N.S.E. ©

### Making SENSE out of the situation!

Use this very simple strategy to help understand and address any and every challenging moment and when the question comes to your mind...is this sensory or behavior? How can I help my child?

## S.  Stop, assess the situation, don't assume it is "behavior"

Try not to simply react, as it is important to analyze the situation to determine if there is a sensory trigger. Do not force the child through the situation. This can create further negative reactions from the nervous system. Also maintaining a calm and objective state of mind will benefit the situation. Children co-regulate via those around them. If you are stressed or angry or panicked, this will create further dysregulation.

## E.  Environment change

Change the environment, even if only briefly. This can help you determine if there is indeed a sensory trigger. It will also give yourself another minute to assess the situation. And when I refer to changing the environment, this can simply be turning the T.V. off in the room, as the auditory input may be too much for the child.

## N.  Note the child's response to the environment change

Notice how the child responds to the change. Watch closely for body language, pattern of breathing, tone of voice, etc. This will tell you so much about the state of the nervous system. If you see a positive change, then you are on the right track. If not, change something else.

## S.  Sensory strategies and tools

Implement sensory strategies right there on the spot...from applying deep pressure touch or a head compression ...or letting your child bury his/her head into your chest while you give a bear hug...or offering a sensory retreat, a squish box, a weighted blanket or noise cancelling headphones. The sensory tool and strategy may also be something as simple as a Camelbak water bottle or encouraging deep breaths. It may also be leaving the group play date a little early if needed. The list goes on and on....

## E.  Embrace the positive and learn from the moment

Embrace the moment as a learning experience and develop more understanding and respect for your child's sensory needs and differences. Do not let frustration get in the way or have thoughts like "how do I fix this" or write it off as another bad experience. Learn from it...respond with respect....and embrace your child for who he/she is and will become. Remember that children simply want to be loved and understood.

# Topic #4
## Sensory Anchors

A sensory anchor is a behavior or repetitive activity which helps the brain organize, calm, soothe, and achieve or maintain ready state. It is a sensory signal indicating that the child is possibly dysregulated or in need of a dose of a "feel good" sensation that is calming and soothing. It can also be an indicator that the nervous system is on the brink of sensory overload or a sensory meltdown. For those with sensory differences, the world can be a scary, unpredictable, disorganizing, and often uncomfortable place. When a child discovers a sensory based activity that feels good, the tendency is to do it over and over. For instance, lining toys up can be visually soothing, similar to looking at spinning objects or following a line with the eyes. Toe walking provides proprioceptive feedback, which can be very calming and regulating as well. We all seek out sensory activities which are soothing and regulating, and children with sensory differences tend to take this to a whole new level.

**A sensory anchor helps the child feel grounded, in control of the moment, and provides a sense of brain organization and regulation. Here are some examples of possible sensory anchors. This is just a short list, and almost any sensory signal you have read about in this book can serve as a sensory anchor for a child, even when found to be maladaptive such as banging the head.**

- Lining toys/objects up
- Following a line or straight surface with the eyes
- Looking at a spinning object
- Hand flapping
- Toe walking
- Making repetitive mouth sounds
- Chewing on a non-food object
- Smelling objects or a new environment/room
- Scripting and repeating phrases
- Rocking or bouncing

# Topic #5

## Fight or Flight

Understanding what fight or flight looks like with a child is CRUCIAL in determining how to respond. The primitive and actual purpose of fight or flight is to divert blood from the brain to the muscles in order to respond quickly and with great strength as needed. For those who over-register sensory input, the brain and nervous system perceives the input as a true threat and the sympathetic nervous system is activated (fight or flight). The unfortunate part is this tends to happen many times a day for a child with sensory sensitivities.

Here are some more examples of what "fight or flight" might look like for a child....

- Kicking, screaming, biting, spitting, throwing things, etc

- A child may try finding any place possible where visual and auditory input are decreased, and where he/she will not be touched or required to make eye contact.

- The child may try to find a cozy and tight space where the body will receive much needed proprioception and deep pressure touch, such as under a table or bed, buried in your arms, or retreating to the corner of a room.

- You may see obvious body language attempting to block out sensory input, such as covering ears, closing eyes, tucking the arms and legs, or curling up in a ball.

- The child may run and try to escape from the situation at hand...without any regard to safety.

- The child may lash out...keep in mind this is not the child being aggressive or intending to hurt someone. The nervous system is doing the talking.

- They child may scream, talk back, call names, cry uncontrollably (also the nervous system).

- It may also present in a much more subtle way, such as "checking out" or zoning out.

- You may also observe a quick change in facial expression and quick shift of mood and emotion...possibly to irritability, frustration, anger, or panicked crying.

Here are some guidelines on the best way to respond....

- Encourage deep breathing...even if you are doing the deep breaths, it is amazing how the child will likely pick up on it and start taking deep breaths. Remember talking to the child or asking the child to do it is not effective. The deep breaths will also help you as the parent feel better. Research indicates that taking deep breaths is one of the most effective tools to bring the brain/nervous system back to ready state and to even avoid fight or flight all together.

- If the child will let you...just hold him/her tightly, providing deep pressure touch in the form of an even pressure bear hug. Do not rub the arm or back or hair, no rocking. Simply be together quietly taking deep breaths.

- Do not talk to or try to rationalize or bargain with the child.

- If a sensory retreat is available, encourage or gently guide the child there, allowing as much time as needed to recover.

- If the child has found his own makeshift sensory retreat (behind furniture or under a bed), leave him alone until he's ready to come out. It may take a while, so be patient.

# Topic #6
## Ready State and Self-Regulation

Self-regulation is the ability to adjust or regulate the level of alertness depending on the time of the day and the stimuli presented. An example of self-regulation is being able to wake up in the morning, become alert, adapt to the school environment and demands placed on the nervous system in the school setting...including attention to task, cognitive demands, communication, social and emotional demands, and motor tasks (gross, fine, and visual motor). Then being able to return home for the evening and prepare the nervous system for rest and sleep. The ability to self-regulate the nervous system involves all of these components, including the sleep/wake cycle. The ultimate goal is to achieve and maintain ready state. Children with sensory differences quite often have a very difficult time with self-regulation due to various reasons. Adapting to the environment, and constantly changing needs and demands on the nervous system requires very complex processing in the brain, which is often taken for granted. When children have a difficult time with self-regulation, we observe maladaptive responses to the environment and sensory stimuli. It is very important to identify these signals of self-regulation before jumping to conclusions that it is behaviorally driven. Depending on the neuro-behavioral state of the brain, the child may need an increased amount of sensory input or a decreased amount of sensory input.

### Dysregulation »»» Co-Regulation »»» Self-Regulation

There is a process in which the brain learns and develops the ability to self-regulate. For those with sensory differences, this process can be so much more difficult, and the amount of time spent dysregulated is much more than the neuro-typical brain. We are taught to help children self-regulate by giving them the sensory tools they may need, and to do so independently. This is strongly recommended and very essential, BUT sometimes the most important step is missed . . . the important step of co-regulation.

Co-regulation is when people feed off of the state of regulation of those around them. And our children are like regulating sponges! They sense it all, and they feel the stress of others. They can also sense frustration, disappointment, and sadness, and they are extremely sensitive to the state of regulation of those around them. This includes if and when a parent is stressed, anxious, unsettled, angry, or irritated (even when it is not directly related to that child). This can also include your tone of voice, speed of talking, pitch in your voice, and body language. Even too much excitement and praise can be overwhelming and create a state of sensory overload...so be aware of this side of things as well. Most children do NOT do well in a rushed, intense, loud, multi-sensory environment...even the sensory seekers. Occasionally this is fine, and completely part of life...but not on a day to day basis. Remember that a child is co-regulating from those around him minute by minute.

Children with sensory differences often rely on those around them to help "co-anchor and co-regulate" and to help achieve and maintain a state of self-regulation. Think of it this way...let's say you are outside in a horrible wind storm, 100mph winds, and the stop sign at the corner is the only thing for you to hang on to keep you safe and from blowing away. Well, this can be how your child may feel...like her world and life is a constant "wind storm"...and YOU are the stop sign. The wind storm is dysregulation, and the stop sign is co-regulation.

It is SO important for us as parents to be that solid rock . . . a stable and calm co-anchor and co-regulator in all situations. Our sensory kids already may see this world as a scary, unpredictable, out of sorts, and sometimes painful kind of place. We need to be that safe place and solid rock they can rely on in challenging and stressful situations and moments.

## Topic #7

### Respect and Understanding is the Key

Now that you have made your way through the handbook, I am sure you have already gained a much greater respect for your child's sensory differences and signals. When you understand why your child is acting a certain way, and that there is likely a sensory root and reason behind it, your response will be different...one that is positive, respectful, productive, and encouraging.

Sensory input is so very powerful...children who seek out sensory input may spend their entire day doing so, just to self-regulate and to achieve and maintain ready state. They may be so preoccupied with getting enough sensory input, that it is nearly impossible to complete other daily tasks and to maintain a stable mood. A child who is jumping on the couch, or hanging upside down, or chewing on the collar of a shirt is doing so to get more sensory input.

On the other hand...a child may avoid sensory input at all cost throughout the day because it is painful and uncomfortable. This may be due to one or more of the sensory systems. For example, auditory and tactile...unexpected sounds or certain tones and pitches may be very painful to the nervous system along with light unexpected touch and different textures on the skin. Finding the right sensory tools for defensiveness is the key to helping children in this scenario. It is also important to assess the environment on a constant basis to determine possible sensory triggers.

## Topic #8
## A Natural Sensory Diet

The brain responds best to purposeful and meaningful activities. A rigid sensory diet/home program is not nearly as likely to be carried over long term as it is to naturally incorporate sensory activities into the day. Sensory needs and challenges can change on a day to day basis. One technique, tool, or strategy may work one day and not the next.

The brain and nervous system respond best to an environment set up with various types of sensory tools that provide different forms of sensory input. The child should have access to these different tools as needed throughout the day…no specific amount of time, in no specific order. The brain and nervous system are constantly processing sensory input and changing on a minute by minute basis, and only that brain (child) knows what it needs at any given moment. So setting up a strict routine or schedule can actually be a disservice. AND the most important part is in the carry over and long term application of all of this…when it is a natural part of the day and becomes a meaningful part of the daily routine (not a strict schedule), you will be more successful! I have heard SO many times from parents that the child resists the activities, and that is because the brain didn't need it at that time. Who wants to be forced into things all day long in the first place?

**What is the number one reason I don't recommend a scheduled sensory diet???**

**Because it lasts for about 3 days.**

**Here are 4 reasons why naturally incorporating sensory activities into the day is best…**

- It will significantly increase your success and long term carryover…this is simply human nature. It should not be stressful. It should be fun, easy, and not forced!
- The theory behind sensory integration is child led and directed, and the brain responds best to purposeful and meaningful activities. A scheduled and rigid sensory diet goes directly against this concept.
- You can naturally incorporate tactile, vestibular, and proprioceptive activities into just about anything you do! (Besides sitting on your rear end and holding or looking at a screen.)
- Guiding and encouraging your child to seek out what the nervous system needs at any given moment in a day is an essential life skill that will be utilized every day for an entire life span.

## Topic #9

### The Power Sensations…The Sensory Foundation

Vestibular, proprioceptive, and tactile input are called the "power sensations" due to the fact that they are the foundation for sensory integration and sensory processing skills. These three types of input provide the basis for brain development (besides the autonomic functions of the nervous system such as respirations and heart rate).

When you work on one area it impacts the processing of the other two in many ways. The complex processing of the brain and the pathways in which these three sensations integrate is the key to success!

Now here's the thing…almost all children with sensory processing differences have difficulty processing information in at least one of these three areas, often all three.

The power sensations are the foundation and root of all development. Incorporating sensory activities from these three categories is essential for all children. And for those children who have sensory processing difficulties, it is critical. This may sound like a daunting task, but it doesn't have to be! When you live a sensory life and set up your home as a sensory friendly environment, it becomes a part of your child's day in a meaningful and purposeful way!

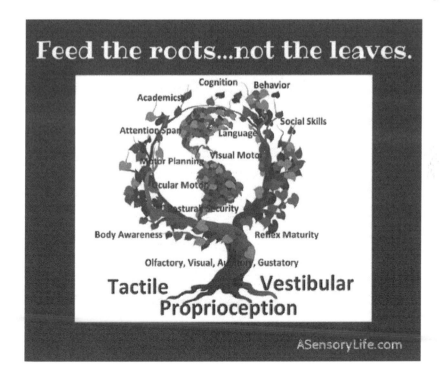

# Topic #10

## Back to the Basics...The Holistic Approach

Sensory input is not enough...it is only one ingredient in the recipe for brain development and enrichment. This topic could be a whole book in itself. I will just summarize and touch on the important concepts. When you take things back to the basics, it really becomes much less overwhelming and makes complete sense! Our brains have not changed...but we have. The bottom line...our society keeps creating and bombarding the brain and nervous system with more and more toxic and unhealthy components. Yet at the very same time the nervous system and brain are being deprived of essential healthy components. Here are my top ten back to the basics tips...

1. Eliminate all processed foods from the diet. Dyes, preservatives, additives, etc. can affect nervous system health in a detrimental way.
2. Stick to whole and organic foods whenever possible to avoid GMOs, pesticide residue, and other toxins, which are also known to cause problems for the brain and nervous system development and processing.
3. Drink pure, filtered water. Fluoride is a neurotoxin and is the number one reason to not drink city water. (Some cities have banned fluoride, you may be one of the lucky ones!). Drinking purified water also eliminates dangerous heavy metals that are also found in the water.
4. Get plenty of sunshine. Sunshine is the natural source of the vitamin D3 which is the most critical and essential vitamin for nervous system health.
5. Connect with the earth everyday (grounding/earthing) with bare feet for at least 15-30 minutes.
6. Eliminate all chemical based cleaners, household products, detergents, air fresheners, etc. from the home and replace with natural or homemade varieties.
7. Eliminate the use of chemical based personal care products, including soaps, lotions, shampoo, etc.
8. Think real hard and long about any pharmaceuticals you are giving your child (unless it is medically necessary)...consider natural and sensory based intervention first.
9. Do not allow more than 1-2 hours of screen time per day.
10. Consider food intolerance and food allergies as a possible root of sensory dysregulation. Be sure to always feed the gut probiotics and other fermented foods as well as address any nutritional deficiencies which may be contributing to brain and nervous system health.

## Topic #11

## Your Go-To Sensory System…Proprioception

Proprioceptive input is the most accepted and tolerated form of sensory input, along with deep pressure touch (a form of tactile input). Proprioceptive input can be regulating, calming, soothing, organizing and/or alerting…depending on the state of regulation and the current needs for the nervous system. That is the beauty of proprioception! It can be helpful at any time. Proprioceptive input occurs any time a muscle and/or joint is pushed or pulled, even with slight resistance. The more resistance (heavy/hard work) the more proprioceptive input. Basically anything besides just laying down or sitting on your rear doing nothing will provide proprioceptive input. Proprioceptive input occurs any time you activate the use of muscles, which go hand in hand mechanically with the joints of the body. The goal is to provide a therapeutic dose of proprioception, throughout the day, as often as needed and desired. This is divided into two types: joint traction and joint compression.

Natural ways to achieve **joint traction** (pull or tension placed on any given joint of the body):

- Climb or hang from a tree, railing, chin-up bar, playground equipment
- Hang from knees hooked over a low bar or railing
- Drape backwards over a large therapy ball, arms overhead
- Hang over the side of a bed
- Stretching activities or yoga
- Resistance band activities
- Pull a wagon or cart
- Carry heavy objects such as a water pail or jug
- Play catch with a weighted ball
- Swing a bat, tennis racket, golf club, etc.
- Any and all sports

Natural ways to achieve **joint compression** (push or weight bearing on a joint)

- Jumping, running, hopping, skipping
- Wheelbarrow walking
- Yoga
- Resistance band activities
- Rebounder, BOSU ball, or trampoline
- Bike riding
- Any and all sports
- Hand stands and cartwheels
- Pushing a heavy box, cart, or other heavy object
- Climbing activities

This is a just a small sample of the MANY ways to get proprioceptive input!

## Topic #12

## The Vestibular and Auditory Connection

The vestibular and auditory systems have a very unique sensory connection. They share a cranial nerve that sends input to the brain. This is the vestibulocochlear nerve. When the brain is receiving auditory input, the vestibular system in being activated, and vice versa. So, incorporating the two into an activity is powerful because when you activate one, the other is ready to rumble!

**When a child is engaged in a movement activity...incorporate listening and auditory processing skills.**

Here are some ideas:

- Play a listening and thinking game such as doing math problems or going over a spelling list
- Sing songs
- Play soft instrumental music in the background
- Play music and sing along
- Use a metronome and follow the beat by clapping hands or using a musical instrument
- Play memory or guessing games
- Play category games

**When a child is engaged in an auditory learning activity...involve movement.**

This applies to in the classroom at school or during schoolwork at home. Do you wonder why some children have a difficult time sitting still during a learning activity? When the brain is trying to process the auditory information and make sense of it, the vestibular system can help and the brain is trying to do just that...move! Therefore, you will see the child trying to get vestibular input via fidgeting in the seat, trying to stand up, rocking back on the chair, bouncing in the chair, etc. **The brain thrives on movement to learn, attend, and process information.** It is unfortunate that our society and educational system has decided that sitting still is the best way to learn.

But there is hope! More and more schools are being educated in regards to sensory needs! Ball chairs, balance boards, BOSU balls, and T-stools are being used in the classrooms instead of regular school chairs. Simply sitting on a ball chair or T-stool activates the vestibular system. You don't have to be bouncing across the room to activate the vestibular system. Give it a try! Replace your office chair with a large therapy ball...I bet you will love it.

For a printable handout to share with your child's school and educators visit:

http://asensorylife.com/ball-chairs-in-the-classroom.html

# Topic #13
## The Screen Time Addiction

- Research on the brain suggests that an **infant/toddler should not be exposed to any screen until the age of three years old**. The brain NEEDS the crucial and critical sensory input of vestibular, tactile, and proprioceptive input to develop a foundation for all of the developmental milestones and higher level skills needed in life (such as academic, language, and social). The visual input received from screen time is NOT beneficial for brain development! So when a little one is in front of a screen/TV, he/she is being deprived of the essential sensory experiences which the brain really needs. The concept of "Baby Einstein" is a disgrace in my opinion. Sure the music part is wonderful...but to encourage a baby to be in front of a screen is a disservice to that baby.

- The average child in America gets **6-8 hours of screen time** a day...probably more. And there are now public service campaigns encouraging one hour of movement a day. It should be the exact opposite!

- **The recommended amount of screen time in a day for any child over 3 years old is no more than 2 hours**...and if your child goes to a daycare, preschool, or public school, it is possible that the child already had 2 hours of screen time before coming home for the evening.

- **We all need the proper sensory nutrition, not just our kids....and we all need to limit our screen time to no more than 2 hours.**

- Without the proper amount of proprioceptive and vestibular input, all of our brains are negatively impacted...not just children with sensory challenges. It affects mood, emotions, the ability to concentrate, the sleep/wake cycle, overall health and well-being, and relationships with others.

### The problem is...our brains haven't changed, but we have.

- Our society has changed SO much and at such a rapid pace, simply leaving no room for the basics and the important stuff for the brain. With technology simply taking over our lives, the important sensory input is pushed aside. And as adults we can tolerate and handle this better...because our brains are finished developing...but our children need to be moving and playing! **Just imagine the negative impact this has on a child with sensory processing differences**.

A good rule of thumb is to at least balance your child's day with the same amount of time in true sensory play as time spent in front of a screen of any kind. If your child spends one hour in front of the computer, then you follow up with one hour of sensory play...preferably involving vestibular and proprioceptive input.

People spend so much money on electronics and gaming systems and such. As much, or more, needs to be spent on creating a sensory environment in the home, such an indoor swing, a BOSU ball, a pillow cave, hippity hop ball, scooter board, etc. For the price of a tablet or gaming system, you can buy ALL of your essential sensory tools!

Play and spend time outside . . . in every season, every single day. It is more than the 3 big power sensations. It is about the fresh air and the sunshine and the true spirit of being a kid.

As the adult and/or the parent, be very aware of this. Join in on the sensory play to get your own sensory needs met too and to spend quality time with your kid! The brain responds best to purposeful and meaningful play.

Challenge your family to decrease the amount of screen time in the day. It's a beautiful thing! So go ahead...start right now. Stand up, look up, and go see what the real world has to offer today.

## Topic #14
## Sensory Modulation

Sensory modulation is the process in which the brain is taking in all of the various types of sensory input and messages and sorting it all out. There is a specific place in the brain called the reticular activating system (RAS), which is like the hub and distribution center for the brain. The sensory information is then sorted out and sent out to the appropriate pathways for different aspects of daily function, self-regulation, ready state, etc.

**Nervous system: The conveyor belts**
**Nerves: The boxes of different types of sensory input**
**Brain: Where all of the boxes are sorted out and stored**

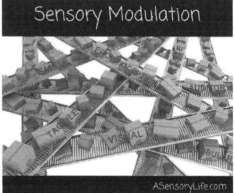

So the boxes are coming in on the conveyor belts one after another, at a nice even pace. At the end of the belt the reticular activating system is nicely sorting the boxes on a constant basis and putting the boxes on the right shelves. This is how the neurotypical brain works.

Those who struggle with sensory modulation will find that the conveyor belt is running too quickly and gets jammed and piles up at the unloading spot. Or the conveyor belt is running REALLY slow and the shelves are empty or almost empty. Sometimes it is as though the conveyor belt has a short in it… starting and stopping, starting and stopping.

To maintain ready state and a state of functional regulation (self-regulation) the conveyor belt needs to be running at different speeds throughout the day such as when waking up and getting going for the day, and then maintaining ready state during the day, then transitioning back to a slower speed at night. And for those with sensory modulation difficulties, the conveyor belt is not efficient at changing speeds at the right time.

**How you can help your child...**

- Lots and lots of proprioception! Proprioception is the key to organizing, regulating, and giving the brain a chance to sort out all of the incoming sensory information.
- Watch for sensory triggers which seem to escalate and cause difficulty, and provide sensory tools and strategies as needed.
- Use tools for defensiveness as appropriate for your child to help decrease the forms of sensory input which are particularly a threat to the nervous system.
- Providing a sensory retreat is a key component to help the child "sort out" all of the incoming sensory messages.
- Focus on the power sensations of tactile, proprioception, and vestibular input to help the brain learn to process information more efficiently.
- Encourage deep breathing on a regular basis and the use of oral sensory tools.
- Be sure to understand fight or flight and respect that children with sensory modulation difficulties will often switch to fight or flight more often and very quickly.

# Topic #15
## The Power of Vestibular Input

Vestibular input (movement and balance) is critical for brain development beginning in utero. Then after birth, it is how we calm infants and also how we make them smile and giggle. We rock them, bounce them, swing them, and sway them. All of this movement is doing a whole lot more than putting them to sleep or making them smile. It is creating a foundation for the brain and development. This need for movement continues throughout life and is especially crucial in the developmental years, but it is essential throughout our lives to support self-regulation.

### Key Points on Vestibular Input and How to Make a Difference

- Everyone should have the opportunity to get up and move every 15 minutes. Even just a quick stretch is beneficial.
- Inverting the head is very powerful and an excellent tool for a quick dose of vestibular input. Visit this link for more information:   http://asensorylife.com/inverting-the-head.html
- Fifteen minutes of swinging can have a 6-8 hour effect on the brain.
- There are 3 vestibules, all which detect and process different planes and directions of movement: back and forth, side to side, rotary, diagonal, and vertical input. It is important to incorporate all of these planes of movement, but allow rotary input only in controlled doses.
- Vertical vestibular input (bouncing and jumping) is typically the most accepted form of vestibular input and is very regulating and organizing since it also involves a great deal of proprioception. Visit this link for more information: http://asensorylife.com/the-incredible-benefits-of-jumping-and-bouncing.html
- Whenever possible, offer options besides sitting in a chair…lying on the floor propped on elbows, standing on a balance board, standing on a BOSU ball, sitting on a ball chair or T-stool, etc.
- Spinning needs to be limited and supervised. This can be very disorganizing for the brain and can cause delayed sensory overload and dysregulation. Monitor spinning and limit to one revolution per second and a maximum of 10 revolutions, then switch directions. This is referring to single point axis spinning. Visit this page for more information on this topic: http://asensorylife.com/the-effects-of-spinning.html
- Respect a child's reaction to vestibular input as it can be very powerful and cause a systemic reaction such as nausea, a headache, flushing of the skin, and even a low grade fever. Stop means stop if the child has had enough. Watch closely for signs of sensory overload, especially if the child is unable to verbally communicate.

# Embrace the Sensory Journey...

**Ready to learn more and live a sensory enriched life?
Take the next step!**

**ASensoryLife.com**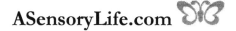